THE ATOMIC CITY
A Firsthand Account by a Son of Los Alamos

Terry L. Rosen

Howard County Library
Big Spring, Texas 79720

SUNBELT EAKIN  Austin, Texas

FIRST EDITION
Copyright © 2002
By Terry L. Rosen
Published in the U.S.A.
By Sunbelt Eakin Press
A Division of Sunbelt Media, Inc.
P.O. Drawer 90159
Austin, Texas 78709-0159
email: sales@eakinpress.com
website: www.eakinpress.com
ALL RIGHTS RESERVED.
1 2 3 4 5 6 7 8 9
1-57168-752-1

Library of Congress Cataloging-in-Publication Data
Rosen, Terry L., 1944–
    The atomic city : a firsthand account of a son of Los Alamos / Terry
L. Rosen.– 1st ed.
        p.   cm.
    Includes index.
    ISBN 1-57168-752-1 (hbk.)
    1. Rosen, Terry L., 1944–Childhood and youth. 2. Los Alamos
(N.M.)—Biography. 3. Rosen, Louis, 1918–Family. 4. Sons—New
Mexico—Los Alamos—Biography. 5. Los Alamos (N.M.)—Social life
and customs—20th century. 6. Scientists—New Mexico—Los
Alamos—Biography. 7. Los Alamos Scientific Laboratory—Biography.
I. Title
F804.L6 R67   2002
978.9'58053'092–dc21   2002152659

In Loving Memory of Jennifer (Polly) Tuck

Jennifer Tuck, circa 1960.

Contents

About the Author

Terry Rosen was born on the campus of Penn State University while his father was earning his Ph.D. in physics. He arrived at Project Y—also known as the "Atomic City," the "Secret City," "the Hill," and Los Alamos, New Mexico—in 1944 at the age of four months, and it was his home until 1964.

After graduating with a B.A. from Colorado College in Colorado Springs, Colorado, Mr. Rosen taught high school social studies in southern Colorado for two years (1966–1968). He then attended the University of Denver College of Law, graduating with a J.D. in 1971.

Mr. Rosen worked as a labor relations analyst for the City and County of Denver from 1972 through 1974. In late 1974 he was asked by Denver's mayor, William McNichols, Jr., to establish an agency to address citizen complaints regarding Denver City and County Government. He agreed to do so and served as the director of the mayor's Office of Citizen Response for nine years. While serving in this capacity, he did considerable public speaking and appeared on numerous TV and radio programs to promote public awareness of "Citizen Response" and, when called upon, to represent the mayor.

In 1977 Mr. Rosen joined the board of the Multiple Sclerosis Society of Colorado and served as chairman for a year beginning in 1984. In 1979 he was made a lifetime honorary member of the Denver Jaycees. In 1981 he was chosen by the Denver Federal Executive Board as Municipal Employee of the Year for the Denver Region.

After leaving Citizen Response in late 1983, Mr. Rosen did business consulting while teaching part-time—public administration at the University of Colorado, Denver campus Extended Studies Program; and Colorado state and local government, American history, and business law at Denver Technical College.

While teaching, Mr. Rosen dabbled in various entrepreneurial endeavors. In 1987 he developed and began producing a new product—souvenir photographic magnets. He believes he was the first in the United States to produce photo magnets as souvenirs, although he was not the first to market them as business cards.

In 2000 the International Library of Photography proclaimed one of Mr. Rosen's photographs, entitled "Winter's Solace," one of the best photos of the twentieth century. In 1994 he began experimenting with a new and unique photographic art form that he calls STAR WRITING™.[1] He had planned to begin marketing STAR WRITING™ in the summer of 1999, until a tragic event inexorably changed the course of his life on April 30 of that year when he saw his life's mate, Jennifer Tuck,[2] killed in a horrific accident.

It was that incident that moved him to write this book.

Foreword

In the midst of World War II, an assemblage of the best scientists and engineers in the world worked in a secluded part of northern New Mexico on the development of an atomic bomb. They brought to this critical project a concentration of knowledge and skills, encompassing many disciplines, unprecedented in history, and very likely unrepeatable. Against the backdrop of a beautiful mountainous environment, enriched by a mixture of Native American, Hispanic, and Anglo cultures and their histories, a modern drama replete with discord, failures, and triumphs—and its own significance for history—was being enacted with extraordinary dedication and urgency.

Terry Rosen tells about his experiences growing up in Los Alamos during the period 1944–64, providing us with parallel coming-of-age stories for a youth and a town born within a year of each other. With sensitivity and humor, he brings us intimate glimpses of the personalities and accomplishments of a number of scientists and their colleagues who lived and worked at Los Alamos during that first phase of the community's existence.

My parents moved to Los Alamos in 1944 when I was nine years old, so I, too, was a son in Los Alamos. The nine-year age difference between Terry and myself naturally meant that I was barely aware of his existence while I was growing up. I viewed much of the same landscape and many of the same people during the period 1944–52 but, of course, through a different lens and from an older perspective. Some twenty-five years later, I returned to Los Alamos and worked closely on a number of physics projects with Terry's father, Louis Rosen, for whom I developed deep, enduring admiration and respect. Much is said in this book about that remarkable person.

My memories and impressions are, if not congruent with, complemented and enlarged by those Terry shares with his readers. Paramount among mine are the accessibility and beauty of the surrounding area with its canyons, forests, and mountains; the playfulness and humor, despite the stress in their lives, of the research leaders when in our company; the virtually seamless integration of the town's children with little attention paid to whether one's dad was a plumber or a Nobel Prize winner—perhaps a special egalitarianism enjoyed only by young children; and our uncertainty and trepidation about entering the "outside" world after the cloistered existence at Los Alamos. I believe the stress, pressure, deadlines, and momentous importance of the project levied an emotional/psychological toll on the parents and wonder to what extent this was passed on to the next generation. Terry examines his feelings connected with that period and how growing up in Los Alamos impacted his personal growth, aspirations, and later life in his second book, provisionally entitled, appropriately, *Fallout*.

Terry's account is at once enlightening and entertaining, illuminating that pivotal period with revealing anecdotes and personal experiences. Those who retain memories and knowledge of that incredible period in Los Alamos are becoming rare. My thanks to Terry for recording happenings and impressions, thereby providing us with a moving and informative kaleidoscopic portrait of a very special place and time.

JAMES BRADBURY

Preface

The "Atomic City" has been shrouded in mystique from its inception. During World War II, many of the world's greatest scientific minds gathered in total secrecy in the remote mountains of northern New Mexico to become the core of the Manhattan Project and usher in the atomic age.

The years I lived in the "Atomic" or "Secret City"—from 1944 to 1964—encompassed the development of the atomic bomb and the hydrogen bomb, the miniaturization of both, and the effort to contain the Cold War. Each of these endeavors required extraordinary efforts by the scientists of the Atomic City.

The Atomic City surveys the background of the Secret City and what it was like growing up there during and after World War II. It also imparts something of the culture of the scientists whom I came to know, and know about, during that time. The sequel, provisionally entitled *Fallout*, is autobiographical in nature and addresses the issue of the long-term impact of growing up in the Atomic City on me, and perhaps others.

I am aware of no other extant book of life in the Atomic City as told from the perspective of one who lived it. Some of the events and my thoughts about them I have shared with no one previously.

The stories that I relate about the scientists of the Atomic City are ones of which I have personal knowledge or have heard repeatedly. Many of them were related to me by scientists and the wives of scientists who worked in the Atomic City during or shortly after

World War II. If a story is well known because it has been published repeatedly, I typically did not include it unless my information suggests that, as previously told, it was inaccurate or incomplete, or because it relates to other aspects of *The Atomic City*.

To refresh my recollections, I have discussed many of the events related with others who were there. I have tried to be accurate and truthful, although I do not always tell *everything*. I doubtless have failed to include some things that should have been mentioned. I'm also certain to have made some misstatements, but none were intentional, and if there is a second edition I will correct as many errors as possible. If you, the reader, can think of anything that should have been included, or see an error, your feedback is welcome. If you have other stories about life in the Atomic City that you feel should be shared, you may send them to the address provided in Appendix IV. Be sure to include possible sources of confirmation of your stories and your address and phone number. Also include a statement to the effect that you authorize me to publish the information. If a second edition proves warranted, appropriate changes will be made and, where possible, you will be credited for your contributions. In the event of multiple submissions of the same story, however, no credit will be listed.

One difficult aspect of writing this book was deciding what not to include. My sincere apologies to those who are not mentioned in the manner they might have preferred.

Finally, do not let the technical aspects of the first chapter dissuade you from reading on. The remainder of the book is much lighter reading.

Acknowledgments

Special thanks to my mom and dad for their substantial contributions regarding the early days of the Atomic City, as well as for their considerable assistance with other aspects of this endeavor.

Thanks to the Good Friends Are Forever (G.F.A.F.) group for helping clarify my recollection of long-ago events: Terry Anna (TA), Bob Bergland (Bob B.), Bob Critchfield, (Critch), Wayne McCloskey (Mac), and Steve Robison.

Thanks to the following for talking with me about their backgrounds and their experiences in the Atomic City: Harold Argo, George Bell, Bill Beyer, Jim Bradbury, Bengt Carlson, George Cowan, Winston and Jean Dabney, Peter Dechert, David Hawkins, Don MacMillan, Kay Manley, Kay Mark, Darragh Nagle, Hugh Paxton, Don Rose, and Françoise Ulam.

Thanks to the following for their many and varied contributions to this project: Elizabeth Allred, Danny Anna, Fabiola Baca, Danny Doss, John and Janis Clements, Sharon (Melton) Lippencott, Kathy Munch, and Roger Meade.

– 1 –

The Manhattan Project

The Atomic City has had a profound impact on civilization—perhaps more than any other community in the history of man. It has also had a profound impact on those who lived there. What was it like growing up there? I'll tell you.

It was Christmastime. I was almost two years old. World War II had ended just four months earlier. "Oh, no! I don't want you sitting on that nasty man's lap!" my mother proclaimed as she whisked me off the lap of General Leslie Groves, head of the Manhattan Engineering District—better known as the Manhattan Project. This one remark speaks volumes about the relationship between the military and scientific communities at "Project Y" during the war. General Groves was playing Santa for the youngest residents of what came to be called the Atomic City. He was handing out candy, but his military bearing prevented him from condescending to wear a Santa outfit. He was not one to be concerned with whether people liked him—only that they got the job done. His reputation for getting things done and his capable leadership were what caused President Roosevelt to select him to head the Manhattan Project—the effort to build an atomic bomb. Overall control remained in the hands of a civilian oversight committee, but Groves was the man charged with putting it in motion.

General Groves (1896–1970) had just completed his last

1

charge—that of building the Pentagon—and was looking forward to his first overseas assignment. Consequently, he was initially disappointed to learn in September 1942 that his assignment had been rescinded and that he would be heading up the Manhattan Project instead. However, once he was told that success of this endeavor could end the war, he warmed to the task. The new assignment also entailed a promotion from colonel to general to provide him with the clout and stature necessary to get things done.

If a professor asked his students to research the identity of the one person who was most responsible for the United States having undertaken the effort to build the atomic bomb, I believe the majority of those students would conclude that it was Leo Szilard. In 1939, with the support of fellow Hungarian refugee Eugene Wigner, Szilard convinced Albert Einstein to write a letter to President Roosevelt expressing the urgent need to begin development on an atomic bomb because of the threat that Germany might already be doing so. Edward Teller drove Szilard to that meeting with Einstein, and Teller said later of that incident that he "entered history as Szilard's chauffeur."

In Hans Bethe's critique of Edward Teller's recently published memoirs, however, Bethe states that Einstein's letter "didn't work." He indicates that it was not until 1941, when the British made a strong argument regarding the possibility that an atomic bomb could be built, that President Roosevelt was prompted to initiate action that resulted in the establishment of the Manhattan Project. I suspect that it was actually the combined weight of both, and perhaps additional factors, that prompted Roosevelt to act.

Despite his key role in initiating the project, Szilard was detested and distrusted by General Groves. This was due to Szilard's opposition to the militarization of the project; his espousal of the need for a unified world government; his vocal resistance to Groves' security measures; and his convictions regarding the need for a free exchange of ideas among scientists internationally. He also mercilessly made fun of General Groves and his military bearing. For example, Szilard might have said, "By order of General Groves, you will complete your theoretical research on the bomb by 1400 hours"; or, "These meetings will continue until we figure out why we're not making any progress." Actually, it was Dick

Feynman who is credited with the latter remark, but it is clearly reflective of Szilard's attitude toward the military.

Szilard was never granted security clearance to go to Project Y during the war. He did visit once or twice, but not until long after the war's conclusion. Once Germany had been defeated, Szilard became one of the loudest voices in the scientific community against the further development of nuclear energy for military purposes. His opposition was fervent, and General Groves felt this vindicated his lack of trust in Szilard.

Over strong opposition from army intelligence, General Groves selected Robert J. Oppenheimer—"Oppie" as he was called by most who knew him—to head Project Y. The objective of Project Y was to complete research and development of an atomic bomb by the time there was enough fissionable material available to produce one or more of them. Opposition to the selection of Oppie derived from the fact that his wife and brother had once belonged to the Communist Party. Indeed, suspicions of communist ties haunted Oppie for the rest of his life. During the war he was constantly being interrogated by one security-conscious organization or another, and well after development of the atomic bomb, he even lost his security clearance for a number of years.

General Groves was responsible for overall security of the Manhattan Project, and he took that responsibility very seriously. The problem was not just to keep the Germans from obtaining information that might be useful to them in building their own A-bomb; there was a very real concern about keeping sensitive data out of the hands of a then-current ally, the Soviet Union. General Groves wanted to make Project Y a military installation and require all scientists to accept commissions as military officers. Initially, Oppie didn't object to the idea; however, when word of the proposal got out, many of the scientists whom Oppie needed to recruit for the project indicated that they would refuse to participate under such circumstances. They were strongly averse to the idea of having to work under such constraints and felt the resulting regimentation would be inefficient and counterproductive. General Groves deferred, and the idea was discarded.

The pressures of the urgency and the importance of the Manhattan Project achieving success were immense. After all, the project would draw tremendous amounts of resources away from other important war-related research projects, such as radar, encryption, decoding, etc. It would consume considerable construction materials, equipment, scarce metals, and, perhaps most important of all, brains. There would be hell to pay if all those resources and efforts didn't produce a bomb and help shorten the war "as advertised" (to President Roosevelt).

For example, electromagnetic plants for separating U^{235} from natural uranium at Oak Ridge required a tremendous amount of low-resistance metal for conducting electricity. Copper was in short supply, so the Manhattan Project borrowed 60,000 tons of silver from the U.S. Treasury. It was done on the sly, in that the Treasury Department never took the silver off their books. That way, they didn't have to explain to Congress where it went. However, every three months, an aide to General Groves had to sign a document confirming that he could still account for every ounce of the silver. Under the agreement between the Manhattan Project and the Treasury, the silver was to be returned to the Treasury within six months after the war's end.[1]

In addition, in order to assemble the equipment necessary to do the research and development at Project Y, it was necessary to borrow sophisticated equipment from various universities. A cyclotron was borrowed from Harvard, two Van de Graffs from the University of Wisconsin, and so forth.

General Groves had been given the impression that research and development on the weapon had been completed and that construction of facilities was all that remained to be done. He was more than a little misguided. After he accepted the assignment, the general learned that he had been charged with constructing facilities for building a weapon that had not yet been designed. Furthermore, he was responsible for overseeing the separation and purification of uranium for that weapon, although no one knew how much purified uranium (U^{235}) and/or plutonium (Pu) would be needed. Only a few grams of U^{235} had ever been purified, and for a bomb, many pounds would be needed. No one knew what separation processes should be used, how large the facilities for these processes would have to be, or how much of what equipment would be needed. It seemed that every time General Groves asked a question, no one had an answer.

All aspects of the project were still in the research phase. The research was being done at the University of Chicago, the University of California, and at numerous other locations throughout the country. In late 1942 Enrico Fermi achieved the first controlled nuclear reaction in the squash courts under the stands at the University of Chicago's Stagg Field. Now it was almost certain that an atomic bomb, with an explosive power that would dwarf any existing weapon, was possible. Just ten or fifteen pounds of U^{235} could release the explosive energy of ten or fifteen thousand *tons* of TNT![2]

However, there was still much research to be done and numerous engineering problems to overcome. It was determined that having scientists working in so many disparate locations would be inefficient, and virtually impossible to control in terms of security. Hence, it was decided that all aspects of bomb development should be brought together in one place.

That place had to meet numerous criteria. For security purposes, it had to be isolated and require little or no relocation of existing residents, because the greater the number of people uprooted, the greater the probability of attracting attention. For security against attack, it had to be at least two hundred miles from either coast. It had to be large enough for the research facility and for the necessary housing. It had to have an independent water supply. It had to have a local pool of available labor. The climate had to be moderate enough to allow work to continue year-round, and there had to be sufficient access to minimize the time-consuming construction of roads. In addition, Oppie felt a pleasing setting would be important for morale purposes, since everyone would be asked to remain cooped up in one place for two years or longer.

In November 1942, General Groves and Oppie went to New Mexico looking for such a site. They first drove from Albuquerque to the Jemez Springs area, but what they found was a narrow valley of insufficient size. Oppie owned a ranch near Pecos, and he remembered his horseback rides up to the mesas[3] east of the Valle Grande ("large valley").[4] He also remembered there was a boy's "ranch school" there, and he suggested that they drive farther to take a look at this location.

The volcanic mesas nestled among canyons covered with piñon and other pines, yucca, cacti, and cottonwoods spread out like a splayed hand from the mountains to create the Pajarito Plateau at an elevation of 7,000 feet. I recall having read or heard that chunks from the same eruption have been found as far away as Missouri. I also heard many years ago that Huerfano Butte, in southern Colorado, came from that volcano. The sides of the mesas are sheer cliffs, many of which are pocked with Indian caves and ruins. Ten miles to the east, at the base of the mesas, the Rio Grande meanders through the Santa Clara and San Ildefonso Indian reservations on its way to Albuquerque and on to Texas.

The site met all of the primary criteria. It was isolated; few people would have to be relocated, yet there were local residents who would be available for hire. Space was sufficient for the research facility and necessary housing. The site had an independent water supply, although it turned out to be somewhat tenuous during the winter. The weather was not optimal, but satisfactory, and there was an existing narrow dirt road.

On the eastern side of the mesa, the road involved steep grades and hairpin turns with substantial canyon drop-offs, sometimes on both sides. There was one such turn that scared me so much, I closed my eyes every time we drove it. I have no idea how big army trucks maneuvered that curve without falling off the road. That curve even challenged the turning radius of our car, and we had to slow down almost to a stop to make the turn. To the west, the road ran across the eastern edge of the Valle Grande with its collage of spruce and aspen trees tracing the edges of the caldera.

As a bonus, there was existing housing sufficient for thirty scientists and support personnel—as many as it was initially thought would be needed.[5] There were half a dozen log houses with bathtubs—later dubbed "bathtub row"—and a number of other cabins. There was Fuller Lodge with several bedrooms and a "throne room," and the "Big House," which could accommodate up to twenty people. Students had lived in the "Big House," but they were expected to sleep year-round on a second-floor porch with only a canvas cover to protect them from the elements—a level of existence that most scientists and their families would not have found acceptable.

Finally, the setting was picturesque and the view spectacular. The local culture would prove alluring and intriguing to the newly transplanted population. For those same esthetic reasons, the site facilitated retention of many of the bright young scientists once the war was over. It also proved of immeasurable benefit in subsequent recruitment efforts. This enabled Project Y to become and remain one of the premier scientific research facilities in the world through the twentieth century and beyond.

Mr. Ashley Pond had established the Ranch School in 1917. He hired a Mr. Connel to run the school, and Connel ran it until the day it closed in early 1943. The father of longtime Colorado congressman Tim Wirth taught at the Ranch School, and Tim has told me that he was born there. According to one alumnus of the Ranch School, Peter Dechert, it was a very good school and graduates were always able to go to the college of their choice. Stirling Colgate, of the Colgate toothpaste family, was a member of the last class to graduate from the school. He returned to the site as a physicist in 1976, after distinguished careers at the Lawrence Livermore National Laboratory and as president of the New Mexico Institute of Mining and Technology in Socorro.

Shortly after the visit by Groves and Oppie, the government purchased the Ranch School, including the horses and schoolbooks, for $440,000.[6] On December 4, 1942, Mr. Connel received a letter from Secretary of War Henry Stimson to the effect that condemnation proceedings were under way for the federal government to assume ownership of the property effective February 6, 1943. I have also read that the school was in financial difficulty and that the governing foundation was more than happy to sell at a fair price. Course work was greatly accelerated so the students could complete the school year, and the school was vacated in February of 1943.

Thus was born Project Y of the Manhattan Project. As soon as the government took over, tanks were brought in to guard both entrances, and they remained there until the Atomic City became an "open city" in early 1957.

The Manhattan Project was almost terminated before it got under way. Renowned physicist Edward Teller raised an issue that most books on the subject gloss over as though it was never a serious concern. In fact, it was critical. The earliest discussion I have found on this issue was between Edward Teller and Robert Oppenheimer in early 1943. As recently as 1991, Teller made reference to the issue in a published article:

Early in the development of the so-called atomic bomb Teller suggested to Oppenheimer that there was a possibility that the first nuclear fission test, code named TRINITY, might ignite the atmosphere and annihilate the human race. This almost led to a cancellation of the Manhattan project to develop nuclear weapons until Konopinski and Teller, in a one-page document [dated December 2, 1943], concluded that the safety factor ... was at least a factor of 60.[7]

That "one-page document" is registered as LAA-01. Thus it may have been the first official document entered in the files of the Los Alamos Scientific Laboratory. The specific issue addressed was: Would the temperatures generated by detonation of an atomic bomb be high enough to ignite the atoms of nitrogen in the atmosphere on a scale sufficient to cause spontaneous ignition of much, or all, of earth's atmosphere? Although the document concluded that there was a high margin of safety, a question mark remained. Might there exist a law of physics of which physicists presently were unaware?

David Hawkins, the philosopher on the staff at Project Y, told me by phone in January 2000 that he suggested to Teller that, regardless of how low the probability of atmospheric ignition, given the impact of error, would it not be wiser not to risk a detonation? Teller, with his wry wit, responded, "Oh, David, there are worse things that could happen."

As the Trinity test did not ignite earth's atmosphere, mankind dodged that bullet. Had we not, there might have been no one left to ask, "What happened?" However, "atmospheric ignition" was not a dead issue. A document dated January 1953 states: "The theory of nuclear forces is still in a rudimentary stage and while it is generally agreed that very large effects of this kind (spontaneous ignition of the atmosphere) are improbable it would be unfortunate if one were mistaken and if one were the cause of disastrous consequences through overconfidence in present day nuclear theory."[8]

I find this statement remarkable for two reasons. First, I think few would disagree that it is the mother of all understatements. Second, and of slightly less significance, its style would suggest that it was written before the comma was invented.

Teller revisited the issue on several subsequent occasions. Upon development of the H-bomb, the first of which was a hundred times more powerful than a Hiroshima-class atomic bomb, Teller felt the initial analysis had been hurried and considered it important to reevaluate the possibility of atmospheric ignition.

Teller hypothesized that the increasing size and efficiency of thermonuclear weapons, and the resulting increased internal temperatures and energy release, increased the probability that a "nuclear tornado" could result in atmospheric ignition. Teller communicated his concern to Soviet physicist A. N. Zaidel, at the Ioffe Institute in Leningrad in 1961, both before and after the Soviets detonated a hydrogen bomb that was twenty to forty times more powerful than the H-bombs the United States had detonated.

As late as 1987, Teller discussed the issue with Andrei Sakharov, the "father of the Soviet hydrogen bomb." Of that meeting, Teller says,

> When I visited with Sakarov in October 1987 to discuss my hypothesis of a nuclear tornado in the atmosphere, he ... stated that his intuition told him it was not possible. However, he recommended that [weapons scientists at U.S. laboratories] use their know-how to evaluate it, but that it would take a team of scientists and even then they might not know.
>
> Sakarov believed such ... studies should be classified, apparently because of weapons codes involved. I believe the experimental study of a nuclear dynamo should be unclassified to permit the give and take of open scientific discussion.[9]

Thus, the issue of atmospheric ignition was not taken lightly. Given that it is now possible to produce H-bombs of unlimited size, is this still a live issue?

Many of us who grew up in the Atomic City have found ourselves playing the role of apologist for what was done there. When I am confronted with that challenge, such as in my teaching of American history, I respond as follows.

Many people, myself included, believe that the development of the atomic bomb had a more profound impact on mankind than any other event in recorded history. Why? For the first time, man had empowered himself to be the instrument of his own annihilation. In addition, the nuclear age has impacted our lives in innumerable ways. Some look upon the United States as an evildoer for having developed the bomb. What were the United States' moral alternatives?

Before World War II, most nuclear research was being done in Germany, and the Germans had access to vastly greater resources of uranium (via the Belgian Congo and Czechoslovakia) than did the United States. Thus, it was a real possibility that Germany would be the first to succeed in developing an atomic bomb. Had they done so, there is little doubt that Hitler would not have hesitated to use it to greatest possible advantage. It was later learned that the Germans abandoned their effort to build the bomb before the end of the war. I have read that, as of early 1944, Hitler ordered that research funds be provided only to projects that could generate usable weapons within six weeks of the time they were proposed.

Japan also considered building an A-bomb during the war but, like the Germans, they decided they couldn't do it in time to change the outcome, so they, too, abandoned the effort. So, if the United States had not developed the atomic bomb, some other country would surely have done so within a few years. Would we have preferred that Russia or some other country had established an early lead in the development of nuclear weapons? Stalin killed more than twenty million of his own people, so it is difficult to imagine that he would have hesitated to use such a weapon on the peoples of other nations. Thus, it is my belief that the scientists who developed the bomb can in no way be held responsible or accountable for its use. The morality of having used the atomic bomb is a more complex issue. This is addressed at the end of the chapter on Hiroshima.

The Secret City

Until 1941, a narrow-gauge train followed the river up and down the canyon between Santa Fe, New Mexico, and Antonito, Colorado. It stopped at the Otowi Bridge to drop off goods for the Ranch School, and the school sent a truck to pick them up three times a week.

A Basque logger named "Shorty" lived in a little house there, on land owned by Maria Martinez ("Maria the Potter") and her husband. Shorty served as watchman for the railroad's cargo, but one day he just disappeared. After that, Maria's son, Adam, and his wife lived there for a short time, but they found it too lonely and moved back to the San Ildefonso Pueblo.

Community is almost as important as family in the culture of the Pueblo Indians. I suspect that has a lot to do with why many Pueblo Indians have difficulty in adjusting to life in a big city. Imagine, if you will, that you live in a quiet village with all of your relatives and that you all routinely look after one another. It has been like that for hundreds of years, but for some reason you decide to leave and go to New York City, where you know no one and no one cares whether you live or die. In a culture so different from yours, would you not feel isolated and alienated? Very likely so.

After Adam moved back to the pueblo, Ashley Pond became desperate for someone to safeguard his goods from the time the train dropped them off until his truck picked them up. While in Santa Fe looking for a replacement, he happened upon Edith Warner. She was looking for a job in Santa Fe and was running out of options. Edith dreaded the prospect of having to go back to Philadelphia to resume her teaching career. She was a small, frail, lone woman, and singularly unfit for the position of railroad watchman, but Ashley offered her the low-paying job and she accepted it.[1]

Once hired, Edith persuaded Adam to ride his horse the two miles from the San Ildefonso Pueblo every other day to load the school's goods onto the truck. Over time, the Indians of San Ildefonso accepted Edith as a good friend. Like them, she had little, needed little, and wanted little in terms of earthly goods. The Indians were her only neighbors, and she respected and appreciated them and their way of life. They respected her determination and her kindliness toward them. During World War II, the train stopped running because the steel rails were needed to produce tools of war. Thereafter, Edith's only revenue came from selling soft drinks and snacks to travelers.

Edith needed help to refurbish and expand her house so she could run a small store and tearoom. Adam persuaded his great uncle, Tilano, to complete the expansion. Tilano had been governor of the San Ildefonso Pueblo, spoke English well, and had traveled throughout Europe and the eastern United States. When Edith told him she was from Philadelphia, he delightedly told her that he had been there. From that day on, he lived in one room of Edith Warner's house.

Edith and Tilano had a close but, so far as I know, platonic relationship. She needed him to help maintain the place, and he needed to be needed. He was old enough to be her father, but she scolded him like a child when he overworked. My family and a number of others at Los Alamos were very close friends with Tilano and Edith, and I always admired the fact that two people from such diverse origins could get along so beautifully as equals. I believe it was Edith's relationship with the Indians that resulted in my developing such a strong disapproval of racial prejudice.

Soon after the Manhattan Project was established, scientists and their families began heading for Project Y. Their first stop was always Santa Fe, and whenever a Santa Fean saw someone who looked lost, they sent that person to see Dorothy "Dottie" McKibbin at 109 East Palace Avenue. She would give them directions or arrange for transportation up "the Hill." She took care of just about everything a newcomer needed.

Until mid-1944, there was insufficient housing at Project Y. Consequently, many people, including my father, had to live in Frijoles² Canyon—now known as Bandelier National Monument—for a month or so until their housing was ready. Accommodations there were rustic: some log cabins built by the Civilian Conservation Corps (CCC) during the Great Depression, and a few tepees.

The only way in or out of Frijoles Canyon was a narrow, winding road on the edge of the canyon that was even scarier than the front road to Project Y. To make matters worse, due to a shortage of gasoline, groups of scientists were ferried back and forth in jeeps driven by submariners who had suffered nervous breakdowns due to the stress of submarine warfare. My father says that some of them trembled constantly and they didn't want anyone to notice, so they drove at excessive speeds on the terribly bumpy dirt roads to make it appear that their arms were in rapid motion because of the road.

One day a wild turkey tried to fly across the road in front of the jeep my dad was in but didn't quite make it. The turkey's only revenge was to break the windshield. The driver picked up the hapless turkey and took it to Dottie McKibben. Guess what was on the menu that night? Dottie's office was in Santa Fe, but she lived in Frijoles Canyon and managed that facility for the army along with all her responsibilities in Santa Fe.

Life in the early days was replete with inconveniences. For security reasons, there were very few telephones, and phone calls were not allowed outside of town. This was easily controllable, as the number of outside lines mushroomed from one, in 1943, to three in 1945. All mail was carefully censored, and residents could not travel more than seventy-five miles from town without approval from the military. The only town of any size within that range was Santa Fe. However, it did allow for travel to the train station at Lamy, fifteen miles south of Santa Fe. This enabled residents to pick up scientists and family members who arrived by train without getting special permission. I'm sure that Lamy was under constant close surveillance by various intelligence services. That would not have been difficult, because Lamy consisted of only the train station, a restaurant with a bar, and an old church.

During the war and for some years thereafter, the streets of Project Y were dirt or mud, depending upon the weather. Except for "bathtub row," everyone lived in temporary housing. After all, it was assumed that the Secret City would exist only as long as it took to accomplish the mission. Much of the housing was prefab, and most of the other buildings were Quonset huts—things that look like huge, half-buried culverts—or uninspiring rectangular buildings. There were two enclosed walkways over Trinity Drive connecting parts of the lab. That was as fancy as it got. Everything was painted putrid army green. However, the lab buildings were equipped with the most advanced pieces of scientific equipment in the world—in most cases the first of their kind—developed, machined, and built at Project Y or borrowed from universities.

For years there was absolutely no crime and no such thing as a locked door in the Secret City (outside of the lab). One day while we were living in our first house—a McKee[3]—my mother went to take a shower, and when she came out, the radio was gone. She noticed it right away, because it had been on. She was understandably incensed, so she found an MP and reported the theft. It wasn't the value of the radio, but the idea that someone would do such a thing at Project Y. Minutes later, they caught the culprit in Omega Canyon. He was in an open jeep with the radio in full view on the back seat. He was surrounded by three jeeps full of armed MPs who arrested him then and there.

It turned out that my father had told one of the two army technicians assigned to his group, Mike Clancy, that he could borrow the radio to listen to the World Series while at work. My father couldn't call my mother to tell her Mike was going to borrow the radio, because there was no telephone in the house. When Mike got there, my mother didn't answer the door when he knocked, so he just went in and took the radio.

In late 1945, we moved into a "Sundt"[4]—a four-apartment complex called a "quad," of all things. My father was just one of many scientists who were fresh out of graduate school, so we were not at the top of the priority list for housing. Enrico Fermi and his family had just vacated an apartment in that quad when they left Project Y after the war. Admittedly, they had been living there only because, when they arrived, Enrico declined the offer of a house on "bathtub row" to make a statement against snobbery.

The thermostats in the quads were often wired improperly. When the people downstairs got too cold, they turned up the thermostat and the heat came on in the upstairs apartment. The upstairs residents got too warm, turned their thermostat down, and the people downstairs got even colder. The result was that, during the winter, there was a constant parade of second-floor residents going outside and shouting at the people downstairs to turn the thermostat down, and vice versa.

There were other problems with the heating system, too. The furnaces had to be filled and stoked by hand, just like steam engines on old trains. The problem was that most of the people who stoked the furnaces didn't understand (or care) how they worked. Their primary concern was to only have to load the furnaces once a day. Thus, the stokers tended to overfill them, and immediately afterward, the furnaces bellowed clouds of black smoke and everyone roasted. Then, in the evenings, it got awfully chilly when the coal began to run low. To make matters worse, it wasn't a certainty that the stokers would even show up each day.

Cooking was another adventure. Everyone had a "Black Beauty" wood-burning stove. It was satisfactory for boiling water or frying rationed eggs, but heat in the oven was so uneven that it was virtually useless.

Then there was the water shortage of 1945–46. A GI was sent into Guaje Canyon to check on the primary water pipe; he misinterpreted his instructions and closed the shut-off valve. Before the mistake was discovered, the water in the pipe had frozen, and for the next three or four months water had to be trucked in from the Rio Grande. In the words of Françoise Ulam, "It was treated with liberal amounts of chlorine, but it tasted of gasoline, diesel fuel, or whatever else the truck had been hauling previously." The shortage lasted until the pipe thawed out in the spring.

As soon as the war ended, permanent housing started going up. In 1947 we were among the first to move into the Western Area, where most of the scientists ended up living. My parents lived there through the end of the twentieth century, though they just about doubled the floor space in the interim, so it hardly seems like the same house.

Not all of the houses had fireplaces, and until the mid-1950s, power outages were not uncommon. Several times when the power went out during extreme cold spells we had a *lot* of people sleeping on our living room floor around the fireplace. I used to really enjoy all the company and always looked forward to the next power failure.

In 1949 the Atomic City was officially named Los Alamos (Spanish for "poplar trees," of which cottonwood is a species). In spite of, and perhaps because of, the Spartan and difficult living conditions, there was a sense of closeness and friendship—almost kinship—among people of extremely diverse backgrounds. It was a truly international community. I suspect that this was, in itself, a nearly unique experience.

Many of the émigré scientists had experienced racial or religious prejudice in Europe before going to Los Alamos. Although not so extreme, they soon found that America was by no means free of such prejudice. Indeed, even the venerable Enrico Fermi was not immune. He (because of his Italian heritage) was once referred to disparagingly by an orderly who was announcing his presence to a general or admiral in Washington, D.C. Los Alamos, however, was different. There was a hearty mutual respect fostered by the commonality of purpose and sense of mission. I'm sure there were some who harbored prejudice, but it was not institutionalized, nor was it countenanced by the community. Dedication and morale generally were very high. It even came to be called the "Los Alamos spirit." Even though the wives and children had no idea what "the purpose" of the project was, they knew it was important.

Despite the constant long working hours and the intense pressures of time, there was something of a population explosion, including the birth of a daughter to the Oppenheimers. When Oppie told General Groves that the medical facility needed to be enlarged because of the increasing number of babies being born, the general urged Oppie to shorten lunch breaks. Oppie didn't comply with that particular request.

During the years of unlocked doors, it was not unusual to walk into the kitchen and find a meter reader checking the electric meters. I have often heard the story of one scientist's wife who, upon leaving the bathroom in the buff, with towel in hand, encountered a meter reader in the kitchen. She put the towel over her head and screamed. He left in a real hurry.

Regardless of the inconveniences, the living conditions in Los Alamos could not be described as harsh. Gasoline and liquor were hard to come by, but there was always sufficient food—especially if you didn't mind the potluck of eating whatever was in the unlabeled cans at the commissary.

Residents of Santa Fe looked upon the people who lived on "the Hill" as weird outsiders, and they weren't the only ones who felt that way. Early on, General Groves had told his men, "What we have here is the biggest collection of crackpots anywhere in the world." Santa Feans had no idea what was going on up on the mesas; a frequent explanation they gave to visitors was that on "the Hill" they were developing windshield wipers for submarines.

Whenever someone from Los Alamos was involved in a traffic altercation or got a speeding ticket, the matter was always "taken care of" without further ado. It must have been a bit disconcerting to law enforcement officers that drivers' licenses of Los Alamos residents didn't indicate the names of drivers; they just said "Project Y."

As a kid, I took it for granted that everyone was friendly toward one another. It was some years before I discovered that people in other places were not quite so friendly. In retrospect, the reasons for the camaraderie were pretty straightforward. It was because whenever you saw people on the street in Los Alamos, it was likely that you either knew them or knew who they were. Even if neither was the case, you knew that, whoever they were, your lives were likely to intersect multiple times in the foreseeable future. You knew further that, if they were adults, they were not unemployed, because there was no unemployment. You also knew that they were trustworthy (because everyone had a security clearance) and that you and they shared a common goal, although only a few of them actually knew what that goal was.

Although I was not consciously aware of it for many years, there was a fairly clear-cut "class system" in Los Alamos. There were the scientists and engineers, the technicians, the members of the business community, the maintenance people, and the military. There was little socializing between groups, although this general rule did not hold quite so true for the military personnel. However, by the time I was socially aware, the military presence in Los Alamos was minimal. Most of my friends in grade school were the children of other scientists, because we lived in close proximity in the Western Area. However, all but one of my closest friends turned out to be the children of nonscientists. I can't speak for the kids of other scientists, but I believe the vast majority of the kids felt as I did—that it made no difference what the other kids' dads did for a living.

This class system did not evolve with any discriminatory intent or malice. It just evolved. There was the "need to know" restriction imposed by General Groves for security purposes. The scientists and engineers had to be especially careful what they said to anyone outside their immediate research group. Then, too, physicists were likely to find talk with other physicists about physics more stimulating than talk with a technician who might be more interested in golf or baseball, and vice-versa. Thus, in a sense, it was the natural order of things in Los Alamos during those security-conscious days. On the other hand, Oppie essentially rendered Groves' edict impotent by insisting that all lab workers including technicians be allowed to attend his weekly colloquia for the purpose of sharing ideas and approaches to solutions to problems.

An example of the "military exception" to the general rule was the friendship between the Dabneys and the Rosens. Jean was a first sergeant in the WACS (U.S. Army Women's Auxiliary) and her husband, Winston, was a master sergeant with the Special Engineering Detachment (SED). Winston, like my father, arrived in Los Alamos in the spring of 1944. Jean had been assigned there a year earlier.

When Jean first arrived, there were no women's barracks so she had to live in the "Big House" for a couple of weeks. Before the war, Jean had worked as a technician for Zenith Radio Company, and the lab needed technicians. Consequently, she was soon assigned to work for Darol Froman in E (Electronics)-Division and after some months was transferred to G (Gadget)-Division—the same division my father was in.

There were only 180 soldiers at Los Alamos when Winston arrived. He was the only person in the orderly room, so he had to do everything himself—the morning reports, transporting sick soldiers to the hospital, and so forth. Before the war was over, there was a contingent of 1,800 soldiers at Los Alamos and Winston had been promoted to sergeant major of the SED.

After dating for a year, Winston and Jean decided they wanted to get married. Jean didn't want to be a war bride, though, so they waited until August 18, 1945, four days after the war was over. Due to the housing shortage, they had to live in separate barracks for six months after the wedding. Winston was discharged in December and went to work for the Personnel Department of the lab.

After the war, the Dabneys lived directly above us in the quad, and they spent numerous evenings playing bridge with my parents. Jean remembers that I always rode my tricycle around and around the bridge table and was often still doing so when the game broke up for the night. They said I was intrigued with "everything army" and they got me an army cot, an army blanket, and a little army outfit.

The Dabneys told me that there were plans to tear down the "Big House" and Fuller Lodge. The "Big House" was demolished but, due to the objections of Jim Tuck, Fuller Lodge was spared. There have been so many additions to Fuller Lodge since then that it bears little resemblance to the original, but it's still there.

There was, and is, an abundance of wildlife around Los Alamos. Deer still roam the town in the early morning and at dusk, eating tulips and other garden delicacies. They also still bed down in our yard year-round. We used to see how many we could spot on the way to and from Bandelier (Frijoles Canyon), and the total was often over thirty.

At least once a year, a family of skunks took up residence under our house, and we frequently enjoyed strong reminders of the fact that we were sharing their territory. Happily, they seemed content to coexist with my dog, Socko, and subsequently with my cat, Ike. Neither of them ever took a direct "hit," despite the fact that the skunks often partook liberally of their food and water.

Bears visit less frequently now, but they were common enough in the early days that etiquette was established for dealing with them. If a bear was found in a tree in your yard, it was your responsibility to bake a chocolate cake and put it at the base of the tree to get the bear to come down so that it could be relocated.

There are innumerable stories about bears in Los Alamos. One night, Carson Mark's neighbor heard sounds outside the front door and thought dogs were getting into the garbage. She grabbed a broom, went outside, whacked the dog on the rear, and yelled at it. It turned around and, yes, it was a bear. She walked back inside but immediately had to lie down for a while. Fortunately, the bear was as surprised as she was and made a hasty retreat, not unlike that meter reader.

In another instance, a family was having trouble with "dogs" getting into the garbage, and despite every effort to secure the lids to the cans, the cans were always open and overturned by the next morning. The husband hooked up a movie camera with a tripwire around the garbage cans to find out how the animals were getting into the cans. The plan worked, and he got pictures of the culprit. It was a bear. It would whack on both sides of the garbage can simultaneously and the top would pop off. I concluded from that incident that in Los Alamos, even the bears were uncommonly intelligent.

– 3 –
&%&##![1] Genius Everywhere!

By the end of World War II, there were hundreds of scientists and a total staff of 3,000 at the Los Alamos laboratory. They came from major universities throughout the United States, from Western Europe, and from Eastern Europe. Many of those who came from Europe were Jews who had fled the menace of the Nazi and Italian fascist regimes. There was a particularly sizeable contingent of scientists from Hungary who were sometimes referred to as the "men from Mars" because of their unearthly brilliance. Not surprisingly, for many years Los Alamos had the distinction of having the highest average I.Q. and number of Ph.D.s per capita of any city in the world, and it probably still does.

During the war, standard procedure at Los Alamos was not to use the preface "Dr." when addressing someone or introducing oneself. There was considerable concern that the Germans might discover that the highest concentration of natural science Ph.D.s in the world had gathered on an isolated mesa in New Mexico. By war's end, the habit was well ingrained, and it is still considered somewhat pretentious to use one's title. In accordance with that tradition, I shall avoid its use for the most part.

Again, for security reasons, many of the top émigré scientists were given code names. Niels Bohr was Nicholas Baker; his son, Aage, was Jim Baker; Enrico Fermi was Eugene Farmer, and so

21

forth. The Bohrs were whisked into the United States under a tight blanket of security. After they arrived, someone noticed that on Niels' luggage was emblazoned "Niels Bohr."

Many of the Los Alamos scientists had philosophical objections to some of the security constraints, especially in regard to not being able to exchange ideas and information with scientists at other labs. After all, the free interchange of ideas had always been key to scientific progress. Everything was strictly on a "need to know" basis. However, only a few scientists refused to work on the Manhattan Project because of those limitations. Although most of them grudgingly accepted the constraints, some took delight in demonstrating how ineffective such measures were.

For example, Dick Feynman put the photo of a dog on his badge for months and was never challenged. In the same vein, Charlie Critchfield and Dick Feynman knew where there was a break in the security fence. They each used to go out through the guard gate, come back in through the break in the fence, and go back out the same guard gate again five minutes later. They would do it over and over, and the guards never questioned them as to how they were getting back in. Some scientists wrote letters in foreign languages, including Chinese, just to tease the censors. These antics did little to foster good relations between the military and scientific communities at Project Y.

There is no evidence that Germany or Japan ever became aware of the Manhattan Project, so it appears that security was reasonably effective, despite its flaws. The leaks that did occur involved Russian agents such as Klaus Fuchs, a German refugee and member of the British Mission to Los Alamos; the infamous Rosenbergs; and noncom technician, David Greenglass, who was Ethel Rosenberg's brother and who is said to have had a photographic memory. As a show of mutual confidence and to avoid the months-long process of conducting background investigations, U.S. Intelligence did not investigate members of the British Mission. Consequently, Fuchs went undetected though he had been spying for the Russians for over a year before he went to Los Alamos. After the war he was caught, tried, and convicted of spying, and was imprisoned until the early 1990s. Due to the efforts of the Russian spies, President Truman's "surprise" announcement at Potsdam that the United States had developed a new superweapon probably did not catch Stalin by surprise. Stalin's reaction, or lack thereof, to the announcement tends to bear this out.

The Scientists

Dick Feynman (1918–88) was perhaps best known for his elucidation of the branch of physics known as quantum electrodynamics, encompassing the structure, properties, and interactions of atoms and molecules. It relates to two of the four fundamental forces of nature—the "weak" (subatomic force) and the electromagnetic force. It does not apply to the "strong" (subatomic force) or to the force of gravity.

Dick was a brilliant theoretical physicist who did not fit the mold of a theoretician. It has been said that a theoretical physicist can figure out why a doorbell isn't working but can't fix it, while an experimental physicist has no idea what's wrong with it but *can* fix it. Well, Dick was always intrigued by what made things tick and how to fix them when they weren't ticking. He made a hobby of fixing calculating machines that broke down in T (Theoretical)-Division. When he started repairing the secretaries' typewriters, the leader of T-Division, Hans Bethe, put his foot down and suggested that Dick's considerable talents could be better utilized elsewhere. That part of the story has been told many times. What is not so well known is "the rest of the story," as Paul Harvey would say. Soon after Bethe's admonition, all of the calculators were becoming nonfunctional, so few calculations were being done, and Bethe reversed his decision.

In addition to being a brilliant physicist, Dick was a superb cryptographer, and when he wrote letters to his hospital-bound wife, he would tear them up into small pieces to give her something to do when she received them. He also had his wife and her father respond to his letters in their own made-up codes, for which he had no key. He would then spend what little spare time he had deciphering their letters. The censors did not appreciate the rationale for these procedures.

Dick was also a gifted teacher and a prolific author. He approached teaching and life with humor, but there was typically a serious lesson in his humor. He had an idea for one theory on which he worked fruitlessly for years. Despite his lack of success, he continued to believe in the validity of the theory. He explained his undying commitment to this theory by saying something like, "It is kind of like being in love with a woman. When you're in love, you tend to overlook the flaws." I have been told that Dick was finally successful in substantiating his "flawed" theory experimentally. As a youth, I had the good fortune to be present on a number of occasions when Dick dined with my parents. He was always so humorous and pleasant that I looked forward to those encounters with great anticipation. Dick Feynman received the Nobel Prize for Physics in 1965.

Hans Bethe (born 1906) was, as I mentioned previously, head of T-Division during the war. He left immediately after the war, and for years he expressed opposition to the development of the H-bomb. However, once it became apparent that a new design was likely to work, and after learning that the Soviets were working on such a weapon, he returned to help with the design work. Bethe was recipient of the Enrico Fermi Award in 1961 and the Nobel Prize for Physics in 1967.

Niels Bohr (1885–1962) is recognized as the "father of atomic physics." Following the German occupation of Denmark, Bohr was spirited to Sweden on a fishing boat and from there to England by plane. Several months later he came to Los Alamos, but he never stayed for any length of time. He served as a consultant of sorts— an exception to General Groves' "compartmentalization and isolation" rules—but I've been told that he never did any work on the actual development of the bomb. He apparently went back to England between visits to Los Alamos, but no one with whom I've spoken seems to know for certain. This is due, at least in part, to the veil of security that always surrounded Bohr's movements during the war. Bohr received the Nobel Prize for Physics in 1922.

Edward Teller (born 1908) was large and energetic. He always walked so fast that others had trouble keeping up with him, and few people ever knew that he had lost part of a leg in a fall from a trolley car when he was a child.

Even before the bomb had been tested, Teller felt it imperative that the United States proceed beyond the atom bomb and develop a thermonuclear weapon—the hydrogen bomb or "H-bomb"—before the Russians did so. I have read that Teller agreed to go to Los Alamos during the war on condition that he would be able to devote his efforts to the development of the H-bomb. For his devotion to this effort, he became known as the "father of the hydrogen bomb." However, Teller's initial plan for the "Super"—the theoretical precursor to the H-bomb—proved on paper to be unworkable. A number of people who were there at the time have told me that it was through innovations in concert with Stan Ulam that the first hydrogen bomb was made to work. Nonetheless, I have heard it said that, when it came to signing patents relative to the H-bomb, Teller was rather irate that Stan signed them before he did.

Oppie and many other scientists believed that the H-bomb would be too powerful to be a useful military weapon. They felt that it would be unconscionable to develop it knowing that its primary purpose, if used, would be to kill as many people as possible (rather than to destroy strictly military targets). In testimony before a congressional committee, Teller stated that opposition to development of the H-bomb was downright un-American. Teller was often perceived as a political hawk, but I think his self-perception was that of a true patriot, and many in Washington shared that view.

Teller's remarks added fuel to the fire of suspicion among the military regarding Oppie's loyalty to the United States. Coming as they did at the high tide of McCarthyism, Teller's statements contributed significantly to the fact that Oppie lost his security clearance soon thereafter, severely damaging his reputation. He was subsequently totally exonerated, and his clearance was restored in 1963, when President Johnson publicly apologized for his mistreatment and bestowed on him the Enrico Fermi Award.

Consequent to the negative impact that Teller's remarks had on Oppie, many scientists refused to work or even talk with Teller for many years thereafter. However, my father was not one of them, and Teller often came to see us when he visited Los Alamos after the war. He also sent us a smoked turkey for Thanksgiving on occasion.

One day Teller knocked on our back door. The door had windows, and when my mother saw him she said, "Oh, my God! Terry, run to the bathroom and take the magazine with Edward Teller's picture on it into your room!" I did as she asked, but to this day, I fail to see the logic of her concern. I myself would not be offended if my face was on *Time* or some other magazine and someone I visited had placed it in a magazine rack in the bathroom. After all, it's probably more likely to be read there than anywhere else.

On another occasion, when I was about ten, Teller was dining with us and I asked him, "What is the single most important factor in achieving success?" Without hesitation, Teller responded, "Motivation." To this day, I cannot find fault with his response.

Initially, Teller was a group leader in T-Division. Teller left after the war and just spent the summer months in Los Alamos thereafter.

Teller lectured extensively and once was asked, "Have you ever committed a security infraction?" He responded, "Yes, but it was the fault of my good friend Louis Rosen." Teller explained that they were in Eniwetok (an island in the South Pacific) for a series of nuclear tests. He bet Ernest (E. O.) Lawrence $5 that, in the analysis of a particular explosion, they would not find evidence of the release of high-energy neutrons.[2] After the test, Teller rushed into the lab and asked my father if he had found any such evidence. The film was still wet, so the analysis had not yet been done, but Teller was obviously in a hurry, so my father "sacrificed" a small piece of the film and analyzed it while Teller waited. The analysis showed that high-energy neutrons had been released. Teller hurried to the airport and waved down an airplane that was already taxiing for take-off. The plane stopped, Lawrence opened the door, and Teller handed him a five-dollar bill. Since his doing so transferred sensitive data, and the airport was not a secured area, the transfer technically constituted a security violation.

Teller was one of the many brilliant Hungarian scientists at Los Alamos. He was a fountain of ideas that required careful consideration and evaluation. During the war, this task fell to Emil Konopinski and Fred "Freddie" de Hoffman. Teller made enormous contributions to national security and was responsible for founding the Lawrence Livermore National Laboratory. Edward and his wife, Mici, were frequent guests at our home during the summers of the early 1950s. Edward was recipient of the Enrico Fermi Award in 1962, and many felt that it was a long-overdue recognition.

Harold (born 1918) and Mary (1919–85) Argo were recruited by

Edward Teller to go to Los Alamos in the summer of 1943. They had been students of Teller at George Washington University and, although they did not yet have their doctorates, Teller wanted them to join him to work on "an important secret project." They knew that if Teller was involved it had to be interesting and exciting, so they agreed to go. By the time they got their clearances, it was February of 1944. Just after Fermi arrived several months later, Teller got the go-ahead from Bethe to commence work full-time on the "Super." Theoretical work on the atomic bomb was essentially complete, and Teller and his group moved to F-Division. According to Harold, "Going to work was very much like going to University. They would go to learn physics every day."

Harold said Teller was extremely good to Mary and him. Teller looked after them and their needs as though they were his children, and they were deeply appreciative of it. After the war, Teller and Fermi went to the University of Chicago to teach, so Harold and Mary went there to complete work on their doctorates.

Mary had the habit of remembering people based on their birthdays. Not long after they arrived, they met Bob Richtmyer—a theoretical physicist and good friend of Teller's. Bob's wife's birthday was halfway between January 11 (Mary's birthday) and January 20 (Harold's birthday), so Mary decided to have a party on Sunday, January 15, to celebrate all three of their birthdays. She invited the Richtmyers and the Tellers. When she brought out the birthday cake and everyone sang "Happy Birthday," Teller beamed and said, "How did you know [it was my birthday]?" None of them had the heart to tell him they didn't know, so it ended up being a birthday party for Edward Teller. So far as I know, Teller was never told the truth about this.

Harold and Mary had lunch every day in the mess hall with a somewhat amorphous group of people. Dick Feynman was a member of this group, and Harold told me that, as Dick was a great raconteur, it was always a pleasure having lunch with him. One day Dick was asked how he met his wife. He responded that he saw a very pretty girl sitting on the beach at Coney Island. He had just bought a new toothbrush, and to catch her attention, he took out his toothbrush and walked past her brushing his teeth. Then he turned around and walked past her again, still brushing his teeth. Once he got her laughing, he introduced himself.

Dick Feynman's wife was hospitalized with a prolonged illness in Albuquerque, and everyone knew that Dick had an exemption from the travel restriction so he could visit her on Saturdays after work. One Monday before the end of the war, when Dick joined them for lunch, Mary noticed Dick was wearing a new ring and lightheartedly asked him about it. He said, "Yes, it was my wife's. She passed away over the weekend." Harold recounted to me, "As you can imagine, it was an extremely poignant moment."

The day before the Trinity test, the VIPs were all bused the more than two hundred miles to the test site. The Argos were not invited, because they were junior members of the staff. However, they were aware of when and where the test was supposed to occur, so they and three other people decided to drive south so they could see it, too. They got some topographical maps of the area and determined the best location outside of the White Sands military reservation from which to view the detonation.

They determined that they would have a direct line of sight to the tower (where the Trinity device was placed) from the top of Chupadero Peak, a few miles south of Socorro. They drove as far as they could and hiked about two miles to the top. They were about thirty miles from ground zero, and they could see lights and the reflection of lights off windshields, so they knew they had line of sight to the tower. Harold set up his camera on a tripod, and they waited all night in the intermittent rain. Well after the scheduled time for the test, they figured that it must have been postponed because of the weather, so they packed up and started back to the car.

They had progressed only a few steps and were looking down to see where they were walking in the dark when, suddenly, the blades of grass were casting shadows even sharper than when the sun rises. Harold immediately got out his camera and set it up again. Then the shock wave arrived. It was strong enough that they knew the test had been successful. Harold was still able to get a photo of the mushroom cloud before the light diminished in the night sky.

They were ecstatic! They were also hungry, so on the way back they stopped at a truck stop outside of Socorro to get a bite to eat. Everyone inside was excitedly discussing the explosion, but of course Harold and his party had to be very careful what they said. They basically just sat and listened.

Frederic "Freddie" de Hoffman (1924–89) and Edward Teller were extremely close friends. Wherever Teller was, Freddie was likely to be there, too. Everyone in the lab had locking file cabinets. Dick Feynman's abilities as a safecracker became legendary, and with his propensity for making mischief, he panicked more than one scientist who discovered someone had unlocked his safe in his absence. Freddie was one of those victimized by Dick's antics. When Freddie confronted Dick about it, Dick simply said something like, "Yeah, they need to improve the locks on those things."

After the war, Freddie became president of General Atomics and later co-founded the Salk Institute. While he was president of General Atomics, he tried to recruit my father with a very generous offer, but the Office of the Director of the Los Alamos Scientific Laboratory (LASL) dissuaded Freddie from pursuing the matter.

Enrico Fermi (1901–54) was among the most brilliant of the brilliant. He was superb as both an experimental and theoretical physicist. He, more than others, was able to assimilate aspects of both fields and conclude with amazing accuracy what the end result would be. As indicated previously, Fermi was given his own division during the war: F-Division.

Fermi developed a method for making estimations which I frequently employ myself. Take, for example, the question "How many auto mechanics are there in San Francisco?" There are so many variables that most people wouldn't even attempt to answer. Using Fermi's technique, you begin by identifying as many of the variables as possible. Then you just guess at the numbers for each variable. Your errors will pretty much cancel each other out, and your conclusion will very likely be accurate within a factor of two. Enrico Fermi was awarded the Nobel Prize for Physics in 1938, and received a special Presidential Award for his contributions to science in 1954.

Stan Ulam (1909–84) was signing his homework "S. Ulam, astronomer, physicist and mathematician" when he was ten years old. He pursued all of these interests throughout his life. Stan met his wife, Françoise, in 1939 while he was lecturing at Harvard and she was a French exchange student at Mount Holyoke. They soon found themselves stranded in the United States, having been made refugees by the war. The Germans had overrun Stan's Polish home-land and were poised to do the same to France.

Stan's close associate, Johnny von Neumann (pronounced "noyman"), recruited Stan for the Manhattan Project in the fall of 1943, but it was January 1944 before Stan and Françoise got their clearances to go to Los Alamos. Stan was curious about the remote place to which they would be moving, so he went to the university library to check out a guidebook on the Southwest. As he was sign-ing out the book, he noticed that a number of his associates had also checked out this guidebook, and they had all disappeared in the re-cent past.

Sure enough, when he got to Los Alamos, Stan encountered all of those scientists who had vanished. I'm sure this scenario was re-peated at many of the universities from which physics, chemistry, metallurgy, and mathematics professors and researchers were drawn to work on the Manhattan Project. When he reported his experi-ence, it immediately resulted in a substantial revamping of security measures.

In July 1944, when Françoise gave birth to their daughter, Claire, the Ulams discovered that under military regulations, Françoise's stay in the hospital was free, but they had to pay a dol-lar a day for the baby. Claire's birth certificate, along with those of all of the other children born at Los Alamos during the war, indi-cates that she was born in P.O. Box 1663, Santa Fe, New Mexico.

Françoise recalled the day that Otto Frisch drove her, Stan, and two other scientists—G. I. Taylor and Joan Hinton—to Oppie's ranch near Pecos. The car got a flat tire, and while the three men discussed how to handle it, Joan, "who had the strength of any ten men," fixed the flat. When she was done, the men were still analyz-ing the problem.

Françoise said: "I am still amazed at how, in such a short period of time, so many people bonded together. The collective effort, the shared experiences molded us into a sort of extended family whose close ties have remained and some even deepened to this day." She also pointed out that, although there were many inconveniences, there were no conditions at Los Alamos that she would have de-scribed as hardships.

Stan was quite a philosopher and understood human nature and human frailties. A constant source of irritation to many scientists in national security laboratories is that while Congress is generous with funding for the development of identifiable weapons, it tends to be parsimonious with funds for basic scientific research. Most people fail to realize that new ideas for technological advances derive from basic scientific research. Stan poked fun at this shortsightedness with the following story.

The setting is his hometown in Poland. The time is the High Holy Days, during which everyone is required to purchase a seat in the synagogue. The service is under way, and the cantor is reading the scriptures. A street person in shabby clothes approaches the doorman and requests to deliver an urgent message to the chief rabbi. The doorman blocks his path, saying, "You scoundrel! You thief! You have no message for the chief rabbi. All you want to do is go in and pray! Beat it or I'll call the police!"

Stan and Françoise left Los Alamos immediately following the war, thinking the lab would probably close. However, in less than a year they were back. Françoise explained, "The appeal of the countryside, the people, and for Stan the fact that the lab passed into civilian hands he trusted, together with the exciting nature of the scientific research being done at the frontiers of science, exercised an overpowering pull." Weighty evidence that Oppie was right about the importance of esthetics in site selection.

In addition to his substantial contributions to pure mathematics and to the concepts of thermonuclear weaponry and nuclear rocket propulsion, Stan was a delightful conversationalist who added greatly to the pleasant interpersonal environment at Los Alamos. As a curiosity, my father said Stan's favorite word was *heuristic* ("to stimulate investigation") and that Stan is the only person he ever heard use the word.

I knew Stan quite well because the Rosen and Ulam families were fairly close, and Stan and I shared a love of chess. He knew many of the grand masters, and when one of them visited him, he often invited me over to play chess with the grand master while the two of them chatted. Stan played a very good game of chess. He usually won the first game when we played, but I often won the second. I noticed that the quality of play of both Stan and my dad always declined after the first game. I suspect they had difficulty focusing on matters other than their work for any length of time. The difference was that Stan knew how to play a good game of chess. I noticed the same effect with the grand masters. They usually won the first game, but not infrequently, I was able to win the second. Neither they nor Stan were ever willing to play a third game.

Jim Tuck (1910–80) first went to Los Alamos in 1944 as part of the British Mission. Jim was a scientific advisor to Winston Churchill during the early years of World War II and had been a protégé of Lord Cherwell (Frederick Lindemann), one of the first scientists to realize that an atomic bomb was not only possible but inevitable. Jim's daughter, Jennifer, had a wonderful photo of Churchill, her father, and several others observing the test of an anti-tank weapon. Jim was instrumental in the development of high explosive lenses to achieve a symmetrically spherical shockwave, enabling the implosion of fissionable materials to achieve a chain reaction resulting in an explosion.

The Tucks went back to England after the war and Jim was expecting to receive a knighthood. However, the government changed and Churchill was no longer in a position to recommend people for knighthood, so Jim never became Sir James Tuck. He did, however, receive the Order of the British Empire (OBE) from the Queen of England in recognition of his work. The award was represented by a certificate signed by the queen and a beautiful solid gold cross. In 1951 they returned to Los Alamos with two children they had adopted as babies in 1948. I was introduced to their three-year-old "twins," Peter and Jennifer ("Polly") when I was seven, although I learned much later that they were adopted and were not twins. The Tucks and my parents were close friends, and they were often at our house. Jim and his wife Elsie were very active in Little Theater and other community activities. The Tucks became naturalized citizens in 1955.

Jim's absent-mindedness was the stuff of legend. Among the august group of General Groves' crackpots, Jim was revered as the "town character." He was six feet, four inches tall, slender, and had an almost perennially disheveled shock of hair. Perhaps his best-known slip occurred when he purchased a camper for his pickup truck. The Tucks lived on a street with inclines of 25 percent or greater, but he did the calculations and determined that, due to the coefficient of friction, the camper would stay on the truck without being bolted down. To everyone's amazement, he was right!

However, one day, after stopping at a traffic light on level ground, he accelerated too rapidly and left the camper in the middle of the intersection. He was not aware of what had happened until the police showed up at his house and told him about it.

Jim was the most unflappable person I've ever seen—even in the movies. He used to sleep in the buff, and once, during a ski trip to Aspen, Colorado, he walked into the dorm after dark (there were no hotels there at the time), got undressed, and suddenly discovered that he was in the women's dorm. He calmly picked up his clothes and left.

At one time there was a plan to fill in the one little body of water in Los Alamos, known as Ashley Pond (technically, Ashley Pond's Pond). Jim was strongly averse to the idea, so he borrowed a rowboat, rowed to the middle of the pond, and vowed to stay there until the plan was abandoned. I don't know how much impact his demonstration had on the outcome, but the pond is still there, and I think Martin Luther King was taking notes.

In the mid-1950s, Jim dug a basement. He had purchased an old barber's chair and wanted to put it in the basement so he could sit, smoke his meerschaum pipe, and think in solitude. The rest of the story is less well known. Years later, his wife called the housing maintenance people and complained that her kitchen floor was sagging. An inspector came out, looked in the basement, came back up, and said to Mrs. Tuck, "I don't understand it. There is supposed to be a large concrete support column under the kitchen, and it's simply not there." The inspector called his supervisor and they both investigated, but they never figured out what happened to that column.

Thirty-five years later, that supervisor walked into the doughnut shop that Jennifer frequented in the morning before work. He knew some of the people sitting with Jennifer and joined them for breakfast. He recounted the story, not knowing that Jennifer was Jim's daughter. The supervisor said they were sure that Jim had done something with the support column to make space for the barber chair, but the whereabouts of that column remains a mystery. According to Jennifer, this is the conversation that followed:

Jennifer: "He buried it."

Housing inspector: "What?"

Jennifer: "He buried it."

Housing inspector: "How would you know that?"

Jennifer: "I'm his daughter."

Housing inspector: "Really?"

Jennifer: "Yes."

Housing inspector (blanching from embarrassment): "Where did he bury it?"

Jennifer: "Right where it was. He dug all around it, let it fall into the hole, and covered it up." The mystery was solved!

I was about thirteen when I began going over to the Tucks' house to play chess with Jim every six weeks or so. He wasn't as good at chess as he thought he was, and I had to be careful not to beat him too badly. I was afraid he might stop wanting to play me, like my father had because I always beat him so badly. When Jim smoked his meerschaum pipe he looked just like Sherlock Holmes without the hat. During our chess games, he would switch back and forth between the meerschaum and several smaller pipes. He used to chew on the stems of the smaller ones mercilessly. The pockets of his sports coats were patches upon patches; at least once every time we played, he put a pipe in his pocket while it was still lit. It was hilarious, but I didn't dare laugh. All I could do was calmly bring it to his attention whenever I saw smoke coming from his pocket. Invariably he would say "Oh, hmm," calmly pat out the fire, and refill the pipe.

My primary reason for wanting to play chess with Jim was that I thought his daughter "Polly" (Jennifer) was an absolute doll. I found her zest for life enthralling. I always went to the Tucks' house with the hope of getting a glimpse of Jennifer and, perhaps, even talking with her for a minute. However, I never got to say a word to her. Many times she saw me, but she never even said hello, so I always left feeling rejected and dejected. Shortly before her death in 1999, she told me the reason she had never acknowledged me on those occasions. Her father had a hard-and-fast rule that no one was to interrupt him when he was playing chess. Yes, it was all an exercise in futility.

Jennifer told me that when Jim saw his first microwave oven, the owner told him that if one put a fresh whole egg in it and turned the oven on, the egg would explode. Jim found this difficult to fathom, so he tried it. The egg exploded and made an incredible mess!

Other such incidents occurred when the Tuck family went to

Europe in 1961–62. They registered Peter and Jennifer in a French boarding school for the year, but they all traveled around Europe before the school year began. Jim had met a Spanish baroness who gave him a map of how to get to her castle. He was determined to see that castle, but when they got to a nearby town, he couldn't find the map. He dug through all of their luggage, and much to Jennifer's embarrassment, by the time he was done looking, the contents were strewn all over the town square. When there was no place else to look, he stood up in total frustration, took off his hat to wipe his brow, and found the map stuck in the hat brim. Jennifer told me that when they finally found the castle, it was in severe disrepair and not at all worth the trip.

Come time for the kids to go to the boarding school, Jim put them on the train and left. After the train left the station, Jennifer's brother noticed that the sun was on the wrong side of the train. They had to get off at the next stop, sit in a train station all night with vagrants and drunks, and take a train in the opposite direction the next day. To make matters worse, Jim had forgotten to give them any money, so the only sustenance they could afford was a ten-cent baguette and a bottle of water.

Although the Tucks lived next to the fifteenth fairway of the golf course, Jim didn't play golf. Sometimes, when golfers hit their balls into his yard, he would meet them at the green and offer to sell their balls back to them.

When I worked in the lab's Physics Division as a "summer student" in 1962, I worked on something called "Scilla IV." It was one of several projects in plasma physics being conducted as part of "Project Sherwood." Sherwood consisted of three groups within P-Division (Experimental Physics). Jim Tuck was the overall head of Project Sherwood, but he had received a Guggenheim Fellowship and was on a yearlong sabbatical in France at the time. He didn't return until August, and his first order of business was to give us a report on his work abroad. What he told us sounded impressive, although I didn't really begin to understand the implications for many years. As I recall, he said that he and his fellow researchers had identified RNA. Indeed, it was the first time I had ever heard of RNA or DNA (which had been identified a few years earlier), and I had no idea what they were.

As brilliant as he was, Jim was a total klutz when it came to working with his hands. Jennifer told me that he was endlessly taking electronic gadgets apart and finding himself unable to put them back together. Upon his return to the lab from sabbatical, I was cautioned to be double sure that I wore my hardhat in the construction area. Our group was assembling two giant electromagnets and connecting them to 216 thirty-gallon oil-filled capacitors stacked three or four high above the electromagnets. The structure was four stories high and looked like it had been made from a giant erector set. Jim loved to come into the construction area and tinker with the capacitors and cables. Sure enough, almost every day he would drop something and everyone would run for cover as the wrench or whatever bounced around on its way to reaffirming Newton's theory of gravity.

Of course, Jim Tuck didn't have a monopoly on eccentricity. One day a well-known scientist was standing in front of his car on the side of the road with the hood up. Winston Dabney stopped and asked if he needed any help. He responded that he just couldn't understand it—that he heard a loud noise, and suddenly the car wasn't steering worth a darn. However, he said he just couldn't find anything wrong. Winston said to the scientist, "Are you aware that you have a flat tire?"

Another example of such vagaries could be observed whenever a forest fire threatened the lab or the town. Even the scientists manned the fire lines, and one of them, who wore shorts and sandals year-round, would fight the fires wearing the same attire.

Although Leo Szilard (1898–1964) did not actually work at Los Alamos, he had weighty bearing on the Manhattan Project throughout, and his work and personality were inextricably intertwined with so many of those who did work at Los Alamos that I consider it appropriate to include him in this chapter. Szilard was one of the most peculiar of General Groves' crackpots. He was also brilliant. I have been told that it was Szilard who first came up with the idea of a hotline between the White House and the Kremlin. After leaving Hungary in 1919, he seldom, if ever, had a home address. He was a wanderer and a thinker, living in hotels and off the goodwill of his associates.

After being instrumental in getting the United States to begin work on the atomic bomb, Szilard later became a leading opponent of the use of nuclear energy for military purposes. He wanted all nuclear weapons to be under the control of a world organization. However, this was not the only subject on which he showed apparent ambivalence. While living in Chicago after the war, he was called for jury duty. He took his responsibility as a juror very seriously. While the jury was deliberating the fate of the accused, several straw votes were taken. The results were always the same—eleven for a finding of guilty and one for not guilty. The one was Szilard. The jury foreman went to the judge and reported that the jury was deadlocked. The judge ordered the jury to try again. The jurors discussed and argued and discussed some more. Then they took another straw vote. The result was eleven for acquittal and one for guilty. The one was Szilard.

Prior to World War II, Szilard once went to the Tucks' house in England for dinner. It became quite late, and the Tucks invited him to stay the night. They told him there was a spare bed in the attic. Elsie gave Szilard a pillow, sheets, and a blanket, and he headed for the attic. He ended up staying for several weeks. At one point, Elsie asked if he found his accommodations satisfactory. He said they were fine but that the bed was a bit uncomfortable. Elsie went to the attic and found the mattress still rolled up in the corner. Szilard had been sleeping on the bare metal springs!

Years later, Szilard was invited to stay the night with the Tellers. He was told his bed was upstairs and he went up to see it. A few minutes later, he asked for directions to the nearest hotel, because he remembered that particular bed was too hard and he didn't want to sleep on it. We will never know for sure, but I suspect he confused it with the bed in the Tucks' attic from many years earlier.

John Manley (1907–90) was one of the first people Oppie recruited. Oppie had been advised that John would be a good person to have on board from the beginning. John was a prestigious scientist and would be very helpful with recruiting other top scientists. This proved to be sage advice. Richard Rhodes, in his superbly documented book *The Making of the Atomic Bomb,* suggests that John might have been recruited by Oppie.[3] However, according to John's wife, Kay, it was Leo Szilard who first approached John and asked if he would be willing to work on a project "that would hopefully have an impact on the outcome of the war." A careful reading of Rhodes' book will reveal that the two versions are not necessarily contradictory. John's initial charge was to help Oppie assemble the best possible people from around the country for the project. John served as associate director to Oppie and as senior advisor to his successor, Norris Bradbury, until Norris retired in 1970.

Kay Manley was almost as full of life as Jennifer Tuck was at the age of ten. She is reputed to have had perfect pitch, and she established and for many years directed the community chorale. At the age of ninety, Kay was still climbing on her roof to clear the gutters of leaves. Kay told me that, when John came home after Fermi's experiment (the first controlled nuclear reaction, on December 2, 1942), he walked in, and after thinking for a moment, said to her, "Well, the world will never be the same."

Norris Bradbury (1909–97) was in charge of assembling the non-nuclear (high-explosive) components for the Trinity test. After the war, Norris became the lab director and, according to my father, "Ran it like probably no one else could have for twenty-five years." Glen Seaborg,[4] an Atomic Energy Commission (AEC) chairman during Norris's years at the helm, gave a eulogy for him that was published in *Physics Today*. Glen said, "A colleague of Dr. Bradbury has said that Robert Oppenheimer was the founder of the laboratory, but Norris Bradbury was its savior." That colleague was my father. Glen Seaborg was awarded the Nobel Prize for Chemistry in 1951. Both Glen Seaborg and Norris Bradbury were recipients of the Enrico Fermi Award—Seaborg in 1959, Bradbury in 1970.

Norris and his wife, Lois, always hosted a party on New Year's Day, and I always wanted to go because Jennifer Tuck was usually there. Lois was an absolutely wonderful ball of fire—always busy, unpretentious, humorous, and always attentive to the needs of others. She was the consummate hostess, and of great benefit to the laboratory because of her capabilities in making important visitors feel at home. She and my mother spent a lot of time together, so I saw a lot of Lois.

Carson "Car" Mark (1913–97) and his wife, Kay, left Montreal to go to Los Alamos in 1945 as part of the Canadian Mission. Canada became involved in the war before the United States did, and Car wanted to help in the war effort. He took several summer courses in what was to become the field of nuclear physics. They moved to

Montreal when war-related nuclear research began there in 1943. They moved to Los Alamos in May 1945, though Car got there before Kay and the children. This was due, in part, to the fact that their diplomatic passports entitled them to a posh level of accommodations on the train that did not, in reality, exist. It was six weeks before the authorities acknowledged this and allowed them to travel coach class to Lamy. Kay said, "The first people we met when we arrived were Mary and Louis Rosen."

Although work on the atomic bomb was essentially complete when the Marks arrived, Car made major contributions to development of the hydrogen bomb. Bob Richtmyer had left following a short stint as director of T-Division, and Car assumed the responsibility in 1947. He remained there until Norris Bradbury retired as lab director in 1970. Bradbury's successor, Harold Agnew, wanted to find a brilliant young physicist to run T-Division. He had some difficulty finding the right person, so Car served as acting director for another two years. Harold wanted Car to move into administration, but Car had no desire to become a full-time administrator, so he left the lab. He then served on the Advisory Committee for Reactor Safety for a dozen years before retiring.

T-Division was involved in many diverse missions, including work in chemistry and metallurgy, as well as physics. Former employees of T-Division have told me that Car was extremely bright and was a very good judge of people. They say further that Car was "the glue that kept T-Division together and on track." Many of the projects initiated in T-Division eventually gave rise to whole new divisions.

The Marks always hosted a wonderful party at Christmastime and, again, I never wanted to miss it because Jennifer Tuck was usually there. According to Kay, Jennifer became close to both her and Car in the 1980s.

George Gamow (1904–68) was a particularly interesting personality.[5] He went to Los Alamos with Edward Teller from George Washington University. Gamow came and went intermittently as a consultant during and after the war—another of the exceptions to Groves' isolation rule. He was extremely gregarious and a highly regarded teacher. I met him in the 1960s when he was teaching physics at the University of Colorado. I have always been a fast walker, but I had a hard time keeping up with George. I have been told that, if a student who wanted to enter the doctoral program in physics couldn't keep up with him while walking, George would not accept the applicant.

George would occasionally go to the lecture hall, where there might be a hundred or more students, and tell them, "I won't be able to lecture to you today, but I will be leaving you in very capable hands." He would begin an audiotape of himself giving the lecture and leave. In 1946 George was the first to present scientific theoretical evidence of the "Big Bang" theory of the creation of the universe that was first theorized by Belgian priest George Lemaître in 1927.

Nick Metropolis (1915–99) was a close family friend. He initially proposed, and was charged with building what was believed to be the second mathematical analyzer, numerical integrator, and computer ("MANIAC") in the world at Los Alamos in 1947. Nick hired a newly graduated engineering student to work on the project, and the new employee was working late one night when a man he presumed to be a janitor walked in. The "janitor" asked him some questions about what he was doing and how he was doing it. He answered courteously. A few minutes later, the "janitor" began making a few suggestions about how he could do it better. To the engineer's surprise, the suggestions made a lot of sense.

The next day, the new employee told Nick about the interloper and suggested that Nick consider hiring that janitor to help with construction, because he really seemed to have a good grasp of the nature of the problems involved. Nick asked the new employee to describe the janitor. After getting a clear description, Nick told him, "That wasn't a janitor. That was Enrico Fermi."

Like so many of the scientists I knew, Nick had a marvelous sense of humor, and it stayed with him to the end. I suspect the general good humor of scientists may have something to do with the fact that no experiment in pure science is a "failure." Each serves as a learning experience and adds to the extant body of knowledge.

Darragh Nagle (born 1919) first went to Los Alamos in 1944. Then, along with so many others, thinking Los Alamos most likely would close, he left right after the war. He spent several years at MIT, in Cambridge, England, and in Chicago before returning to Los

Alamos in 1956. Coincidentally, he was working at Project Sherwood when I worked there as a summer student in 1962.

Darragh said Fermi had a standing order that, whenever anyone in Marshall Holloway's "critical assembly" group was doing an experiment, everyone else was to leave the building. Thus, about once a week, they found themselves going hiking during the workday. I find it interesting that this policy for the protection of the workers was instituted by Fermi and not by the lab.

About a week before the Trinity test on the Jornada del Muerto ("journey of death") desert at the White Sands test site, one of the men in Darragh's group was run over by an army six-by-six truck. However, the sand was so soft that he wasn't hurt in the slightest. Darragh was obliged to call the man's mother and report the accident. When he did so, he started by telling her that her son had been run over, instead of first stating that her son was uninjured. Before he could finish the sentence, he heard a "thud" on her end of the line. Fortunately, she had only fainted.

Immediately after the Trinity detonation, Fermi wanted soil samples collected so it could be determined what proportion of the plutonium had been converted to energy by the blast. Herb Anderson was the leader of a group that was assigned to carry out experiments Fermi wanted done, and he took the first tank to ground zero about four hours after detonation. Technicians had removed the tank's turret and lined the bottom of it with about two inches of lead. Then they built a lead-lined compartment inside the tank for the scientists. Herb reconnoitered the edge of the crater and took soil samples.

Darragh took in the same tank an hour later and went into the crater to get soil samples. He had rigged up a periscope so the scientists could see the surrounding landscape, but the blast had turned the sand to talcum-powder consistency, and when the tank went into the crater it stirred up such a cloud of the stuff that they couldn't see at all. Their position had to be triangulated by remote observation posts and radioed to the tank. They got to the bottom of the crater, opened a small hole in the bottom of the tank, used a posthole digger to get their samples, and got out of there as quickly as they could.

A bit later, Julius Tabin took the same tank back into the crater for additional soil samples. Later still, George Weil took another tank to a point 2,000 yards from ground zero. George had tethered some rockets to his tank. His plan was to fire the rockets into the crater and get soil samples while dragging the rockets back to the tank, thus avoiding the hazards of going all the way to ground zero. However, the rockets missed their target, so the experiment was unsuccessful. Even Fermi went out in one of the tanks. I asked Darragh if he felt that the safety of personnel was but a secondary concern at that point. He responded, "Maybe tertiary" (below secondary level of importance).

Darragh said Fermi also employed another technique to determine the efficiency of the blast. He related the well-known story about Fermi tossing small pieces of paper in the air when the shock wave from Trinity arrived. From the angle of declination and distance traveled by the paper, he was able to estimate the yield of the Trinity device. His estimate proved to be amazingly accurate through analysis of the soil samples collected after the blast. The popular version of the story implies that Fermi knew innately how to translate distance and angle of declination of pieces of paper into blast yield. However, I have read that Fermi carefully prepared for the experiment. Thus, he knew in advance what various distances and angles of declination would mean in terms of blast efficiency.

George "Kisty" Kistiakowski (1900–82) succeeded Seth Neddermeyer as leader of the HE-(High Explosives) group. Duncan McDougal had been a student of Kisty's at MIT and, while there, Duncan took Kisty's wife away from him, or so it was perceived. They all ended up in Los Alamos, with Duncan working for Kisty. One night at a party, a longtime friend of the Kistiakowskis approached Mrs. McDougal and said, "Good evening, Mrs. Kistiakowski." She said, "Not anymore. It's McDougal." He said, "Oh! Pardon me! My mistake." She responded, "Oh, no! My mistake."

In his youth, Kisty was an officer in the White Russian Army (loyal to the tsar). Thus, he was strongly motivated to escape from Russia when the tsar was overthrown. He developed a very negative attitude toward the military, and his standing joke was that "All armies are stupid, and the least stupid one usually wins."

On August 14, 1945, when the news came of Japan's surrender, there was a nationwide celebration. In Los Alamos it was a real blast, with hard partying and Kisty setting off copious quantities of

HE. After the war, Kisty became the scientific advisor to three U.S. presidents, beginning with Eisenhower.

Charles Critchfield (1910–94) first went to Los Alamos in 1943. He was a theoretical physicist and worked on whatever project Oppie designated. After some months, he was assigned to head up a group to work on the "initiator," before it was known that the initiator would be the critical key to the functioning of the plutonium bomb. In later years, when someone would credit Charlie with the success of the device, he would always reply, "It was Rubby Sherr's idea that made it work."[6]

The Critchfields and the Rosens were close friends as far back as I can remember. Charlie's son, Bob ("Critch")—one of my closest friends—was one of the first children born at Project Y (in 1944). The Critchfields left Los Alamos in 1946, returned for a year in 1952, returned again in 1961, and stayed for good. Charlie and my mother played a lot of golf together, and Charlie's wife, Jean, often went along for the ride.

Much of the information that follows about Robert Oppenheimer comes from Charlie Critchfield. Charlie's office was very close to Oppie's, and Oppie often called Charlie in for long talks. Oppie would talk not about physics or the bomb, but about the mysteries of life. He would go on and on as though he were lecturing a class, though Charlie was the only one there. Thus Charlie probably knew Oppie as well as did anyone in Los Alamos. To enhance my knowledge and understanding of Oppie, Bob Critchfield loaned me a tape of a talk given by his father, entitled, "The Robert Oppenheimer I Knew."

Robert Oppenheimer (1904–67) was perhaps the most broadly educated of the scientists at Los Alamos. He had studied Eastern religions and taught himself Sanskrit, simply to satisfy his intellectual curiosity. He is also credited with having first theorized the existence of phenomena later dubbed "black holes."

According to Charlie Critchfield, the secretary of a navy captain at Los Alamos had a boyfriend in the navy. One day the boyfriend called her and said, "If you'd like a case of good scotch, I can get one for you. Just send me fifty dollars." Since that was a lot of money, and because there was legitimate concern that the scotch wouldn't get by the army guards who inspected all incoming packages, the secretary asked Charlie if he would like to go in with her fifty-fifty on the scotch. He agreed, and the process was put into motion. The money was sent and the scotch was shipped, disguised as "Globe Ink."

When the scotch arrived, Charlie, Oppie, and Kisty shared liberally in one of the bottles in Charlie's home. At one point, Kisty said, "Everyone calls me 'Kisty,' and I don't like it! I want to be called George." Oppie then said, "Everyone always calls me 'Oppie,' and I don't like it because it sounds too much like the Dutch word for ape. I would prefer to be called Robert." Although Charlie didn't mind his nickname, he didn't want to be left out, so he said, "Everyone always calls me 'Critch,' and I would rather be called Charles." Thereafter, the three always called each other by their proper names.

Kisty didn't really know his way around Los Alamos yet. Furthermore, all lights had to be out by 10:00 P.M. and it was a dark night. By the time he was ready to leave, he had consumed a lot of the Hudson Bay. He stood up, said good night, opened the door, and walked into the closet. He came out, said good night again, opened another door, and walked into the bathroom. When he came back out, Charlie offered to walk him home. Kisty responded, "I can get hoom by myshelf," and staggered out the front door.

Oppie's wit is elucidated by his favorite prayer: "May the Lord preserve us from the enemies without and from the Hungarians within." Most people thought it was funny, but years later, when Charlie told Edward Teller (a Hungarian) about the prayer, Teller said soberly that he had never heard Oppie say that. Then he said, very seriously, "He must have been talking about Leo Szilard." Charlie conceded that was a possibility.

Charlie pointed out that in one respect, most books and movies about Los Alamos are wrong. They suggest that Seth Neddermeyer was unsuccessful in developing a technique for initiating an implosion device. He said that although refinements, such as the "lenses" and shaped charges suggested by Jim Tuck made it more reliable,[7] Seth was actually fairly successful. When it was decided to go in the direction Seth had been researching, Oppie increased the manpower of that research group from six to well over a hundred, and that's when he replaced Seth with Kisty as group leader.

Charlie said that, as the Trinity test date approached, Oppie became depressed and increasingly apprehensive about whether the bomb (specifically the initiator) was going to work, and he lost a lot of weight. Upon detonation, Oppie's first words were, "It worked!" Then he made his renowned statement: "I am become death, the destroyer of worlds." This proclamation derived from his knowledge of the Hindu god Vishnu. After the Trinity blast, Oppie became still more distressed and even lost his voice for about two weeks.

When Charlie was asked whether he, himself, had any regrets about having worked on the bomb, he said he always felt that a scientist has to do whatever he can to support the society that supports him. He explained that the scientists were constantly told that the Germans were ahead of them on development of the bomb. Despite this, Charlie said some of them had misgivings about the work they were doing.

Oppie enjoyed the theater, and whenever possible he would attend the Little Theater productions, most or all of which were produced by John Mench. Oppie would have liked to participate, but he didn't have time to rehearse. Consequently, when producing *Arsenic and Old Lace*, John cast Oppie in the part of a corpse.

About six months before his death, Oppie visited Los Alamos and Norris Bradbury asked my parents to host a cocktail party for him. My father said this was the only time he ever had the opportunity to talk with Oppie at length. Years later, a writer asked my father his impression of Oppie, and my father's response was: "Oppie had the heart of a poet and the brain of an Einstein."

Oppie's brother, Frank, was also a fine physicist, and although he never worked at Los Alamos, he served as the chief administrative aide to Kenneth Bainbridge for the Trinity test. I find this rather peculiar considering the grief that intelligence agencies gave Oppie about the fact that his brother had once belonged to the communist party.

Fred Reines (1918–99) was an exceptionally quiet and gentle man. His daughter and Jennifer Tuck were very close childhood friends. Fred and his charming wife, Sylvia, were bright lights in the community. Fred had a marvelous baritone voice and sang the lead in numerous light operas, most of which were directed by Kay Manley.

During the war, Fred worked with Dick Feynman on estimating yields for nuclear weapons and on hydrodynamics calculations. After the war, Fred was the technical director for the "Greenhouse" series of nuclear device tests at Eniwetok. One of these tests, code-named "George," was the first detonation of thermonuclear fuel. Its success validated the Teller-Ulam idea for producing an H-bomb.

When he got back to Los Alamos, Fred resolved to undertake an experiment of great importance to our understanding of nature—to substantiate the existence of the "free neutrino," the most elusive of all subatomic particles. Enrico Fermi christened the neutrino in his seminal paper on the "Theory of Weak Interactions." *Neutrino* is an Italian word meaning "the little neutral one." It has no charge, no magnetic properties, and essentially no mass. It is so elusive it can only be observed indirectly through its collision with an electron or its transmutation of a stable nucleus into a radioactive one. The probability of such an interaction is so slight that a neutrino is highly likely to pass through the entire earth without any interaction whatsoever.

The planning for the endeavor was done at Los Alamos, and Fred and his colleagues sometimes met at our house to discuss strategies on how to conduct the experiment. They finally decided to mount a major effort to detect free neutrinos that are born in reactors from the fission process. Fred assembled a small group from T-Division and P-Division, and they set up their detectors at the large nuclear reactor at Savannah River, Georgia. After six years of arduous effort, they were finally successful. Due to his work on the neutrino, Fred Reines received the Nobel Prize for Physics in 1995. At the Nobel proceedings Fred remarked that, were it not for the untimely demise of Clyde Cowan, the Nobel Prize probably would have been given to both of them.

When Johnny Williams (1908–66) first arrived at Project Y, he worked out of the director's office as a "troubleshooter" but soon became the director of P-Division. For the Trinity test he was the alternate to Kenneth Bainbridge, who had the overall responsibility for the test. Once, during a seminar, Oppie was speaking and the lights went out. The power plant had failed. Then and there, Oppie directed Johnny to take charge of the power plant. There were no more electrical outages as long as Johnny was at Project Y. After the war, Johnny resumed teaching at the University of Minnesota.

Due to a health problem, Johnny became restricted in how much he could carry, so he became expert in packing light for long trips. He would wear a wash-and-wear suit and take only a briefcase or a small suitcase with spare underwear and socks. He showered every day and would begin fully clothed, wash his jacket and remove it, wash his shirt and pants and remove them, and then wash himself. The clothes were dry and ready to wear again the next day. He and his wife, Vera, spent many Christmases at our house in the 1940s and 1950s. Johnny became leader of the Nuclear Physics Division of the AEC—the organization responsible for overseeing all U.S. nuclear programs from 1946 to 1974—and subsequently became a member of the commission.

I have never known a kinder, gentler person than Bengt Carlson (born 1915). He first went to Los Alamos with Carson Mark and George Placzek from Montreal as part of the Canadian Mission, in May 1945, to work in T-Division. Initially Bengt, his wife, Julia, and their son, David, lived across the street from us, but after a few years they moved to Tesuque (in the valley between Los Alamos and Santa Fe). Julia was instrumental in the establishment of the Santa Fe Farmers' Market, and it continues to flourish today. The Rosens and the Carlsons remained close throughout life.

Bengt was soon made group leader of a computing group.[8] After the exodus of scientists from Los Alamos in 1945 and 1946, he took over leadership of two computing groups. In the latter part of 1946, he left to look at other job possibilities, but after four months he was asked to return. After the Russians detonated their first atom bomb in 1949, his two computing groups were consolidated and strengthened, becoming the Los Alamos Computing Center, which Bengt steered for the next twenty years.

By that time, Los Alamos had one of the largest assemblages of scientific computers in the world, and computing had expanded to division status. In 1957 Bengt chaired a computer design committee that worked with representatives of IBM and other computer companies to advance the art of hardware logic and develop software to implement it. In 1968 Bengt took over a group to focus on the field of "neutron transport theory"—the work he had wanted to pursue when he first went to Los Alamos.

Johnny von Neumann (1903–57) was one of the famed brain trust from Hungary and is recognized as the spiritual "father of the (programmable electronic) computer." In 1956 von Neumann and Ernest Orlando Lawrence were the first to receive the Enrico Fermi Award from the president of the United States.

Most people believe that the first modern computer—ENIAC (electronic numerical integrator and calculator)—was built at the University of Pennsylvania in 1946 by von Neumann. However, some suggest that the first, dubbed "ABC," was built several years earlier by John Atanasoff and his graduate assistant Clifford Berry.

During World War II, the British established a top-secret facility at Bletchley Park (BP) near London, code-named "Ultra," to work on deciphering German codes. Alan Turing, previously an assistant to von Neumann at Princeton, developed the Turing Machine at BP in mid-1941. This machine, considered a computer by some, succeeded in deciphering the German Enigma code. It could also be argued that the "Colossus," developed by Thomas Flowers, an employee of the British postal service, while working at BP in early 1944, was the first programmable computer. There will likely never be consensus on which was the "first computer," because of differing perceptions of what constitutes a computer. Colossus succeeded in deciphering the German Lorenz codes.

Ultra probably saved millions of lives by providing the Allies with invaluable information on numerous military campaigns. However, in 1946, the English decided to destroy all evidence that Colossus ever existed. "That decision almost robbed Colossus of its rightful place in history as the world's first programmable electronic computer."[9] Furthermore, the British didn't release any information about BP until thirty years after the war ended. By that time, ENIAC, MANIAC, and subsequent generations of computers had been much publicized in the United States.

Johnny Wheeler (born 1911) was a physics professor at Princeton and consulted with all segments of the Manhattan Project. Shortly after the Hanford Separation Plant started up its reactor, it had to be turned off to make some adjustments. Twenty-four hours later, when they tried to turn it on again, nothing happened, and they couldn't figure out why. Johnny was called in and identified the problem. Johnny devoted many years to astrophysics, and it was he who coined the phrase "black holes" to describe the collapse of stars into themselves as first theorized by Oppie.

Seth Neddermeyer (born 1907) was, for a time, group leader of the HE group. My father has told me that, for some reason, Oppie didn't particularly like Seth, and Seth never got proper credit for developing the implosion concept. That has been called one of the significant injustices of Los Alamos. Neddermeyer received the Enrico Fermi Award in 1982, in part for his contribution to implosion technology.

Emilio Segré (1905–89) was a student of Fermi's and went to Los Alamos to work in F-Division. At one point, Fermi noticed that Segré was not showing up for work on Saturdays and he asked Segré why. Segré explained that he was spending Saturdays fishing. Fermi asked Segré if he didn't think it more important to be at work with so many important problems to solve. Segré explained that catching fish was not so easy—that it was a real challenge. Fermi responded, "I see, it is a battle of wits." Segré received the Nobel Prize for Physics in 1959.

Isador Isaac (I. I.) Rabi (1898–1988) was working on radar at MIT when Oppie asked him to be the associate director of the new lab. Rabi declined. He "thought radar more immediately important to the defense of his country than the distant prospect of an atomic bomb. Nor did he wish to work full time ... to make the culmination of three centuries of physics a weapon of mass destruction." [10] Eventually Rabi did become a consultant at Los Alamos—another exception to General Groves' "compartmentalization and isolation" rules. Rabi was awarded the Nobel Prize for Physics in 1944.

Emil John Konopinski (1911–90) was, as I mentioned previously, one of the two physicists at Project Y whose primary responsibility was to evaluate Edward Teller's ideas during the war. It was Konopinski who weighed the probability of a nuclear detonation igniting part, or all, of earth's atmosphere and determined that "the safety factor ... was at least a factor of 60."

Victor Weisskopf (born 1908) was among the many Jewish scientists cloistered in Copenhagen prior to World War II to avoid the Nazi menace. Unlike many of his relatives and colleagues, "Vicki" avoided Nazi persecution for the most part, but he couldn't get a job. Around 1936 he was awarded a Rockefeller stipend, but to make ends meet until he received the funds, he took employment in Russia for eight months. He came to the United States in 1937, and he left a teaching position at MIT to go to Project Y. Vicki was known as the "Los Alamos Oracle," because he could estimate any nuclear cross-section, even if no experiment had yet been done to establish it. Shortly after the war, Vicki returned to MIT. Vicki received the Enrico Fermi Award in 1989.

Don Macmillan (born 1913) attended the University of Chicago "laboratory school" from grade one through graduate school—something few, if any, others can claim. When Don was in high school, Arthur Compton, 1927 recipient of the Nobel Prize for Physics, was his Sunday school teacher.

In 1939 Don was teaching chemistry at Cornell when he went to a physics colloquium. Upon its conclusion, highly regarded physicist Robert Bacher[11] got up and told about a meeting he had just attended in Washington, D.C. He said he had learned that, in Germany,[12] Lise Meitner and her nephew, Otto Frisch, had just "discovered fission." He added that, if a self-sustaining chain reaction could be achieved, it would mean a weapon could probably be built. Don heard nothing more about the discovery for years (because following that meeting, the scientific community voluntarily agreed to maintain secrecy on the issue). When the United States entered the war, Don went to work at the Naval Ordnance Lab in Washington, D.C., where he degaussed ships (eliminated the magnetic fields around the ships to help them elude German mines and magnetically fused torpedoes).

In 1942 Don visited Chicago and went to the university barbershop for a haircut. He renewed acquaintance with the barber, who told him that when he wasn't cutting hair he was building Geiger counters for the "Tube Alloys Project" (the British code name for the investigation of the weapons potential of atomic energy). Then, in late 1943, Don was walking with his supervisor and another associate, both of whom were physics professors at Cornell. His supervisor, who was also his friend and roommate, said, "Well, we'll be leaving in a couple of weeks for New Mexico." Suddenly, all of the pieces began to fit and Don knew where work on an atomic project was being undertaken. He also knew that he, too, wanted to go to New Mexico to work.

Don knew that Arthur Compton must be involved, so when he went to Chicago for Christmas, he went to Compton's house, knocked on the door, and when Compton answered, he told Compton that he would like to help on the project in New Mexico in any way he could. Without a word, any sign of recognition, or change in facial expression, Compton said, "Thank you," closed the door, and there was no further contact between the two. Don then went to the Manpower Commission in Washington, D.C., and applied for a job "in New Mexico." He was hired, and when he got to Los Alamos in May 1944, he ended up working for the same friend—the nation's leading expert on high-intensity x-rays—for whom he had worked at the Naval Ordnance Lab. They were researching design aspects of "the initiator"—the neutron source that starts the fission process in the bomb—and were trying to get an x-ray image of an implosion.

Don said that Charlie Critchfield and Jim Tuck were also working on the problem, and that Jim is credited with having resolved it. This was something other than Tuck's idea for the "lens" approach to achieving implosion and is still classified, so Don couldn't elaborate further. In a brief conversation with Don shortly after acceptance of his idea, Jim said: "The trouble with you Americans is that you tend to become enamoured with the equipment, and not with the object of the experiment. We [English] try to go directly to the object by whatever means available, sealing wax and string if that is all we have." Don said he has borne this in mind ever since. In the post-war era, Don was a group leader in the weapons program for many years, and for many more on the Rover project—the effort to develop a nuclear-powered rocket engine.

Don also tells how Kisty, who was a skiing enthusiast, took scraps of HE and drove around the ski hill clearing large rocks by blowing them up. I have read that Kisty also wrapped explosives around trees and detonated them to complete the clearing.

Don was a figure skater and helped develop and run the Los Alamos skating rink for many years. In 1961 he founded the Los Alamos Figure Skating Club. They immediately applied for, and received, membership in the United States Figure Skating Association. He didn't stop skating until one of his knees gave out in the mid-1980s.

Joe Fowler was, like my father, fresh out of graduate school when he went to Los Alamos. From 1946 to 1951, Joe was leader of the cyclotron group and my father was the alternate. As my father put it, "We had a marvelous time making new discoveries in nuclear physics every day." One time they needed to have an interior wall torn down in their lab to make room for a piece of equipment. The carpenter's union said it was their job, but the electrician's union said it was their job. There was no end in sight to the squabbling between the unions, so Joe and my father tore the wall down themselves. Their solution almost caused a strike, but at least they were able to continue with their work.

There were numerous other gifted scientists at Los Alamos, such as physicists Jerry Kellogg, P-Division Leader for many years in the post-war era, and his successor, Dick Taschek.[13] In addition, there were the scientist fathers of the children who were my classmates, but it would be impractical to try to list, much less discuss, all of them. Suffice it to say that if you walked around town you couldn't avoid seeing a scientist unless you were blind.

Due to the shortage of housing, people were often hired because their spouses could also contribute to the project. This meant that two positions would be filled while requiring only one house. Darol Froman, associate director under Oppie, was hired in part because his wife, Ethyl, was a trained pharmacist; and Harold Agnew, who became director of LASL[14] after Norris Bradbury, was initially hired in part because Oppie needed the extraordinary secretarial skills of his wife, Beverly.

Of course, my father knew all of the aforementioned scientists, but I was too young to remember the ones who left right after the war, some of whom came and went as consultants. Notables include

Luis Alvarez (1905–89), recipient of the Nobel Prize for Physics in 1968 and the Fermi Award in 1987; Eugene Wigner (1903–95), recipient of the Fermi Award in 1958 and the Nobel Prize for Physics in 1963; and Owen Chamberlain, joint recipient of the Nobel Prize for Physics with Segré in 1959. There were Edwin McMillan—the group leader in G-Division of the group in which my father worked—recipient of the Nobel Prize for Chemistry in 1950; and Felix Bloch, recipient of the Nobel Prize for Physics in 1952. There were metallurgist Cyril Smith and chemist Eric Jetty, and the list goes on.

In addition to the scientists he recruited, Oppie also hired a philosopher to write a history of the war years at Los Alamos. I mention this because it gives insight into Oppie's persona. The first philosopher Oppie hired didn't stay long, because he had high school–aged children and there was initially no high school at Project Y. The second person, David Hawkins, with whom I have spoken, wrote what he describes as a "technical history of Los Alamos." Oppie also hired an artist, Bob Davis, whose wife was also an artist. I found no one who knows what Bob did for the lab, although my father thinks that he devoted much of his time to editing technical papers. Bob left Los Alamos shortly after the war and subsequently became the editor of *Physics Today*.

Once Germany had been defeated, some scientists objected to continuing work on the bomb, but despite growing discord, work continued unabated. President Truman wanted to use the atom bomb as a hammer over Stalin at Potsdam, and the military wanted to use the bomb to avoid having to invade Japan. Following the success of the Trinity test, an even greater number of scientists expressed opposition to using the bomb.

However, it was not a decision that was theirs to make. They had built the bomb. Now it was up to those in government to use it responsibly. It is up to each of us to decide whether or not the decision made was the right one.

Where Did You Say We're Going?

Of all the Los Alamos scientists, my awareness of one greatly exceeds the level of my knowledge of the others. That one, of course, is my father, Louis Rosen. I provide a more in-depth look at his career because, in many respects, it provides a window into the "flavor" of Los Alamos and the nature of the careers of many of the Los Alamos scientists.

In December of 1941, my father was working on his doctorate at Penn State, and following Pearl Harbor he went to the Navy Recruiting Station in Philadelphia to enlist. However, he failed the physical because he was too thin, so he returned to his studies. His brother, Bernie, tried to enlist in the army, and he, too, was rejected because he was too thin. Bernie was more persistent, though. He walked out, consumed a lot of bananas and water, and then convinced the army to weigh him again. This time he passed the physical and was allowed to join. After the war, Bernie rose through the ranks of the Federal Civil Service to become executive director of the Civil Service Commission at a time when the federal government had more than two million civil service employees.

In late 1943, an emissary of the President's Office of Scientific Manpower sought out my father and recruited him to work on a secret project that would "end the war." He quickly completed his doctoral thesis, and with my mother and me in tow, journeyed southwest in a 1936 Ford.

On the way, they met my mother's dad, "Papa Terry," in Memphis, Tennessee. Papa Terry took my mother and me to stay in Tuscaloosa, Alabama for a few months because there was not yet sufficient housing available for families at Los Alamos. For several weeks, my mother had no idea where my father was. Finally, she was contacted by a government agency and told to go to 109 East Palace Avenue, Santa Fe, New Mexico. She and I flew to Dallas, Texas, but once there we were bumped from the plane to make room for a general. After considerable effort, she got word to my father that we were stranded in Dallas. Telling no one but his immediate superior, my father violated the travel restriction and drove to Dallas to pick us up.

For the next several years, my parents and I lived with several thousand other people in the very crowded P.O. Box 1663, Santa Fe, New Mexico. I understand that the Santa Fe postmaster initially thought the family who had that post office box was extremely wealthy because of all the things they ordered from catalogs.

As was true of all of the early housing at Project Y, our first two apartments were within walking distance of the main lab. There were a number of "firing sites" some distance away, but government jeeps were available for transport from the main lab to the remote sites. Our first apartment was several blocks from the lab, but our second one was just around the corner, about a block away. Consequently, when my father couldn't take time to go home for lunch, my mother would take some sandwiches to him. The guard always insisted on inspecting the sandwiches. What might she have been trying to smuggle *into* the lab? I guess we'll never know. More to avoid this ridiculous intrusion than to avoid the walk, she sometimes just met my father at the fence across the street from our apartment and squeezed the sandwiches through the wire to him.

The other alternative for lunch was the military mess hall, but my parents seldom availed themselves of that option. It was free for GIs, but it cost civilians forty cents for breakfast and fifty cents for lunch. It was only sixty-five cents for dinner, but my parents didn't go out to dinner much either, because they would have to get a babysitter and my father only earned $280 a month (standard for a new Ph.D.).

Occasionally, my parents did get a sitter and go out in the evening. My first babysitter was a GI firefighter. I've been told that he used to take me to the firehouse and let me play on the fire engines. It sounds terrific! I wish I remembered it. When I was a bit older, my babysitter was usually Elsie Pierce, a sergeant in the WACS. She was a good friend of the Dabneys and soon became a good friend of ours.

My father is the greatest man I have ever known. He has become an internationally renowned nuclear physicist and has more common sense than anyone I've ever met. He is well rounded in his knowledge on a multitude of subjects, except for sports, about which he is totally ignorant but for one fact. He knows about "the coach," Bear Bryant. Both the University of Alabama and Penn State University have recognized my father as one of the most distinguished alumni in their history. He has also received honorary degrees from a number of other universities. His sense of humor is truly remarkable. He is a master at defusing stressful situations with humor and can make it difficult for the angriest of people to avoid cracking a smile.

While I was growing up, none of us kids knew what our dads did at the lab. You just didn't ask. Not infrequently, government agents visited us and questioned our dads about one colleague or another, so we knew that this secret business was serious. The scientists who worked on the bomb still have in their heads a lot of classified information, so questioning them about what they did remains a bit tricky. I did not learn until years later that my father worked in G-Division on "implosion technology" during the war. All I knew previously was that he worked on the development of the atomic and hydrogen bombs. Immediately following the end of the war, G-Division was disbanded and my father transferred to P-Division.

During the war, in addition to working on their assigned projects, each scientist was allowed to conduct a research project of their own choosing. Most, including my father, chose to work on some idea related to the bomb project. My father's project involved the frequent detonation of substantial quantities of HE. Consequently, he often found himself sitting in the back of a jeep with twenty to fifty pounds of HE on his lap, bouncing like crazy over extremely bumpy roads on the way to the detonation site. Of course, he is not the only one who undertook such endeavors. Indeed, such risks were considered routine at the time.

Although he submitted weekly reports on the status of his "personal project," my father thought no one was paying it any mind. Consequently, he was pleasantly surprised when he learned that Hans Bethe had taken note of his work and that the results of his experiments proved important in helping to confirm that the Trinity test should proceed.

Until I was about fifteen, my father worked from twelve to eighteen hours a day, often seven days a week. He also frequently flew to the South Pacific for bomb tests for weeks or months at a time. After that (except for the year we lived in Paris), his hours at the lab declined somewhat, but I'm not sure that any of the scientists were aware of the concept of a forty-hour work week.

From 1945 until 1949, when the Soviets detonated their first atomic bomb, and again from 1952 to 1960, after work on the H-bomb had been completed, my father was involved in pure scientific research. The lab officially cut back from a six-day to a five-day work week during those times, but he continued to put in long hours. He worked with highly complex equipment, such as the cyclotron and the Cockcroft-Walton, to expand understanding of nuclear reactions. He pioneered the investigation of the strong nuclear force involving the "spin" of atomic nuclei. He also devised a way to generate a polarized beam of protons using the cyclotron, and this opened up a new field of scientific investigation.

About all I knew was that my dad, like Dick Feynman (and many others), didn't fit the mold. He both understood how things worked and how to fix them. He was so good at it that, whenever anything broke or stopped working, my mother or I would say to the other, "Daddy fix" (meaning, "Don't worry about it, Dad will fix it").

Many people are aware of the fact that, following World War II, Wernher von Braun was one of many German rocket scientists who agreed to work for the United States. The Germans were ten years or more ahead of the United States in rocket research, and von Braun and his associates made major contributions to our missile and space programs over the next several decades. Of course, many other German scientists were captured by the Russians at the end of World War II and subsequently made major contributions to the Soviet missile and space programs. The U.S. Army captured the German rocket research center at Pennemünde before war's end, but by agreement with the Russians it was turned over to them in the aftermath of Germany's surrender. Prior to the turnover date, the Pentagon ordered that 100 V-2 rockets be removed for transport to the White Sands test site. I'm not sure how many were actually shipped before Pennemünde was turned over to the Russians, but some of the missiles made it to White Sands.

Some of the pure research in which my father was involved between 1945 and 1949 involved working with Darol Froman, the lab's associate director at the time, on the analysis of cosmic radiation. Initially, they conducted their experiments with reusable balloons. They would launch a balloon, follow its movement, and recover it (and their data) when it landed. However, once the V-2s arrived from Germany, they began using rockets instead. The rockets went much higher than the balloons, allowing them to learn more about the atmosphere at higher altitudes. They wanted to find out if cosmic radiation would precipitate fission in U^{235}. They were using minute quantities of U^{235} for their experiments, but the military was extremely concerned about the possibility of someone else getting their hands on any U^{235}, so everywhere my father and Darol went with their experiment, an armed military security guard went with them.

In preparation for one nuclear test in the South Pacific after the war, my father told me they had a number of large pieces of equipment called "neutron collimators" to unload. These things weighed tons, and when they transferred the first one from the ship to a raft, the raft tipped over. That collimator is undoubtedly still at the bottom of the bay. Fortunately, they had a spare.

Immediately following another test in the same series, my father, John Allred[1], and their "monitor" (a person whose job it was to constantly watch the radiation counter) were driving toward ground zero to recover their instrumentation. The monitor asked, "What happens if this truck breaks down out here?" John responded, "I'm out of here like a jackrabbit and you're on your own." The monitor was visibly shaken by his response.

You have probably heard of the "Van Allen Belts"—bands of radiation that circle the earth. One is a band of protons and electrons that circles the earth at an altitude of 2,000 miles ± 1,500 miles. The other belt is at an altitude of 11,000 miles ± 6,000 miles. Prior to sending astronauts into space, it was important to know the energy and intensity of these protons in order to determine if they would be harmful and, if so, how to shield astronauts from them.

In the late 1950s, the air force was testing the first intercontinental rockets. The rockets didn't have warheads, so there was some empty space in the nose-cones. LASL got the air force to let them use the space in some of them for experiments prepared by my father's group in P-Division to investigate the Van Allen Belts. The air force also air-conditioned the nose-cones so the heat of reentry wouldn't damage the proton detectors. The experiment established that the protons in the Van Allen Belts were, indeed, of sufficient energy and intensity to pose a potential hazard to astronauts.

In 1960 my father began developing a proposal for a half-mile-long meson-producing "linear accelerator." By 1968, he had convinced Congress to commit $55,000,000 to the project, and construction began. The facility became operational in 1972 and was named the Clinton P. Anderson (Los Alamos) Meson Physics Facility (LAMPF), after the New Mexico senator who was so important in getting the funding through Congress. LAMPF was built on time and under budget—almost unheard-of for such a complex, one-of-a-kind government project.

The existence of mesons—subatomic particles that do not exist in nature—was first theorized by Dr. Hideki Yukawa (1907–81), the first Japanese Nobel Laureate in physics. Pi (π)-mesons, or "pions," demonstrate the transformation of energy into mass. There are positively charged pions and negatively charged pions. These are comparable to the matter and antimatter of Superman comics and *Star Trek* renown. LAMPF was built to invigorate the science of nuclear physics, and it did so in a big way. Once operational, LAMPF was made available to scientists from all over the world. For many years it was the largest nuclear science research facility in the world in terms of the number of users, as well as in terms of beam power. It continues to be an important magnet scientific research facility today, drawing hundreds of scientists from different nations to Los Alamos to conduct experiments.

On June 25, 1970, the *Santa Fe New Mexican* republished the cover story that originally appeared on August 7, 1945—the day after the atomic bomb was dropped on Hiroshima. Excerpts of that article are reprinted in the next chapter. In that same newspaper was an article about LAMPF, construction on which was nearing completion. Following are excerpts from that article:[2]

Written especially for The New Mexican by Dr. Louis Rosen, director of the Los Alamos Meson Physics Facility.

A little more than a quarter of a century ago, our nation was engaged in a fierce war against the most powerful array of totalitarianism ever assembled. Los Alamos Scientific Laboratory [LASL][3] was brought into being for the task of involving nuclear energy on the side of freedom. That task was successfully accomplished.

Almost ten years later, our country found itself in a race with the USSR towards the explosive release of thermonuclear energy. LASL was the spearhead in this encounter. Again success was achieved.

During those years, and the ones following, LASL has discharged its responsibilities in the area of nuclear armaments and has thus played a vital part in maintaining the defense posture of our country at an acceptable level and within tolerable costs.

The world situation does not, unfortunately, yet permit substantial relaxation of our defense activities. These must continue. However, more and more our society's priorities are shifting towards peaceful use of science and towards the solution of vexing problems of energy generation, biology and medicine, and environmental control as well as towards the acquisition of fundamental knowledge. It is, therefore, not unnatural for LASL to now assume a leading role in this aspect of science and technology. A major and recent LASL entry in this arena is the Los Alamos Meson Physics Facility (LAMPF). LAMPF is a facility based on a linear accelerator, much of it invented and developed at LASL, which will carry more power in its primary beams than is available from any accelerator now in existence or under construction. It will accelerate protons, the nuclei of hydrogen atoms to energies up to 800 million electron volts ...

At this energy the protons, when they interact with targets of any material, will produce small bundles of energy which appear as short-lived particles known as pi-mesons. Pi-mesons are believed to be the messengers of the nuclear forces. It is these forces which make possible the great stability of atomic nuclei and the great violence of nuclear reactions.[4]

The objective of all basic research is to deepen our insight into natural phenomena. In a laboratory such as LASL, we have the additional responsibility of discovering how to utilize that enhanced insight, and the technologies developed to achieve it, for practical purposes.[5]

And so, as a result of unstinting support by a brilliant director, Dr. N. E. Bradbury, and of a farsighted and influential U.S. Senator, Clinton P. Anderson ... LASL continues to pioneer into the unknown, opening new windows through which to view nature so that we may better use our resources and our environment towards more comfort, better health and a fuller, more enlightened life.[6]

Shortly after LAMPF became operational, a scholarly-looking older gentleman appeared in my father's office. He introduced himself as Professor Nakimura. He explained that he had been Dr. Yukawa's first graduate student, and Dr. Yukawa had sent him to find out what LAMPF was planning to do with "his" (Dr. Yukawa's) Pi-mesons in the field of medicine—especially in regard to the treatment of cancer. My father explained the potential promise of pions in that area, and that the clinical trials would be conducted under the auspices of the National Cancer Institute. He also invited participation by Japanese oncologists in those trials. Upon his return to Japan, Professor Nakimura was instrumental in persuading Tokyo's largest newspaper to sponsor several Japanese physicians to participate in the clinical trials.

Shortly after the war, Enrico Fermi had returned to the University of Chicago. He built a cyclotron there, and when he first saw evidence of the presence of mesons indicating a large energy release when they stop, he purportedly remarked, "This is the way you should treat cancer." In 1974 a cancer treatment center was established at LAMPF. Only volunteer terminally ill patients were involved in the trials, but most of them benefited from the therapy, and some experienced significant remissions of their cancers. An integral and enduring part of this endeavor was the establishment of the Cancer Research and Treatment Center at the University of

New Mexico (UNM). This center was responsible for evaluating patients to determine if they were appropriate candidates for pion therapy. The center then designed and carried out the treatment, using the LAMPF pion beam. Once treatment was completed, the center was also responsible for conducting patient follow-up.

These experiments precipitated the development of two additional pion therapy facilities—in Vancouver, Canada, and in Zurich, Switzerland. It also stimulated interest in the development of other particle beams for the treatment of cancer. Although somewhat less effective in terms of minimizing damage to healthy tissue, electron, proton, and heavy ion facilities are far less expensive to build, and this has resulted in a large increase in the number of people who can be treated and helped. In addition, the UNM Cancer Research and Treatment Center remains operational and has been a boon to the entire region. In recognition of my father's role in establishing the center, the University of New Mexico awarded him an honorary doctor of science degree in 1979.

In 1965 my father was seeking congressional support for funding the construction of the Meson Facility. In one of his papers promoting the facility, he pointed out that someday it would become necessary to maintain competence in nuclear weapons technologies without benefit of nuclear testing and, when that day arrived, LAMPF could serve as a vehicle for doing so. In 1997 the mission of LAMPF changed, and it is now doing just that. Its name has been changed to the Los Alamos Neutron Science Center, or LANSCE, and it is presently an important component of the "Science-based (nuclear) Stockpile Stewardship program." From 1972 to the present, the Meson Facility has been a major "magnet" facility for drawing scientific researchers to LANL, thereby maintaining the intellectual vitality of the laboratory.

From 1966 to 1985, my father was a member of the USA–USSR Joint Coordinating Committee for the Fundamental Properties of Matter. This committee participated in an annual exchange of non-classified scientific information with Soviet scientists and developed plans for experimental collaboration between the United States and the USSR. This information exchange was established on the premise that it would enhance "confidence-building" between the two countries, thereby reducing the risk of nuclear holocaust and paving the road for the reduction of nuclear stockpiles. The teams took turns traveling to the country of the other team for their annual meeting, so my father made nearly a dozen trips to the Soviet Union in that capacity.

He has also made many trips to the USSR which were unrelated to the Joint Coordinating Committee. On one occasion, he took my mother and my thirteen-year-old son, Terry Lee. Terry Lee took his skateboard with him and skateboarded all over Red Square. The Russians had never seen a skateboard. A few months later, I noticed a story in the newspaper to the effect that a shipload of skateboards was on its way to the Soviet Union. I have no doubt that it was as a direct result of Terry Lee and his skateboard.

Due to my father's numerous visits, he became extremely knowledgeable about conditions in the Soviet Union prior to the fall of the Berlin Wall. Following each trip, he had to submit a report to someone, such as Department of Energy Intelligence, regarding the people with whom he had spoken and what had been discussed. He also often advised members of Congress on his perceptions of the USSR following his trips. When it so happened that I was teaching a college course in history or government at the time he and my mother visited Denver, he would talk to my class about his visits to the USSR. Some of the experiences he related bear repeating.

My father explained that the very existence of the collaborative meetings of the Joint Committee was kept confidential so that, in times of high tension between East and West, neither side would have to be concerned about losing face by allowing them to continue. He said there were only two times that the continuity of the meetings was seriously threatened. The first was when the Russians invaded Afghanistan. The United States' team was already in Frankfurt, Germany, en route to Russia, and the president of the United States ordered them to stop. However, the scientific advisor to the president convinced him of the importance of allowing the meeting to proceed as scheduled and the president rescinded his order.

The other time the meetings were threatened was when the Russians exposed the United States for placing mines in Nicaraguan harbors at a time when the official position of the U.S. was that we were not involved in that area in any way. Again, the president of the United States wanted to cancel the meetings, but after being informed of the importance of the continuation of the meetings, the president said, "Okay. Tell them they can go ahead and meet, but tell them not to say anything." After some hours of silence by the U.S. team, the meeting recessed. During the recess, one of the Russian scientists took my father aside and said, "Dr. Rosen, it appears as though on this occasion you [the U.S. team] find yourselves in the position that we usually find ourselves in."

Due to the fear of possible defections, the Soviet team included their top scientists when the meetings occurred in Russia but included only second-echelon scientists when the meetings were held in the United States. In the 1980s, as trust between the United States and the Soviet Union improved, my father pushed the envelope and tried to get the Soviets to allow a top-flight scientist to come to Los Alamos for meetings. That scientist was Sergei Kapitsa, the son of Soviet Nobel Laureate in physics Pyotr Kapitsa.

After many months (the State Department didn't agree to the visit for six months), the Soviets agreed, and my father made arrangements for Kapitsa's trip from JFK to the airport in Albuquerque. However, on the day Kapitsa was supposed to arrive, there were no Aeroflot flights scheduled to JFK. Finally, my father received a call from Kapitsa. He had come on an unscheduled flight with one other person. He apologetically explained that in the USSR there are some people who do not fly alone, and that the decision to allow him to come was conditional upon his being accompanied by a Dr. Liebermann. Dr. Liebermann had reasonable credentials as a physicist and was the son-in-law of the famous Soviet dissident Andrei Sakharov. However, Liebermann was a known KGB agent. Consequently, the State Department went ballistic when they heard he was with Kapitsa and refused to give permission for Leibermann to go to Los Alamos.

To avoid scuttling the whole effort, when Kapitsa and Liebermann arrived in Albuquerque, Leibermann was put on another plane and sent to a physics conference in California for a few days. Since that time, Sergei Kapitsa has made at least one additional trip to Los Alamos—without Dr. Liebermann or any other companion.

In the early 1980s, my father was invited to the People's Republic of China (PRC). My mother accompanied him and they traveled extensively throughout China. My father gave a number of lectures at scientific laboratories and was asked by the Chinese to meet with Vice Premier Fang Yi. His scheduled half-hour meeting lasted over ninety minutes.

During their meeting, the vice premier explained that he had been given responsibility for education, science, and technology though he himself had never even finished high school. He said, "I am a round peg in a square hole."[7] He said it was imperative for China to catch up with the West in science and technology, and he asked my father, "What would you do if you were in my position?" My father answered that he would identify some of the brightest young scientists in China, send them to centers of excellence around the world to learn, and upon their return, teach what they had learned. Fang Yi replied, "Professor Rosen, that is an excellent idea. Would Los Alamos Laboratory be willing to accept some of these people?" My father responded that, if he received a list of nominees of qualified scientists, he would see what he could do.

My father said he didn't expect to hear anything further but now suspects that the suggestion he made was what Fang Yi had been fishing for during the meeting. After a few months, he received a list of qualified Chinese scientists from the vice premier.

The problem was that the national laboratories had a security-inspired policy against allowing scientists from PRC to visit for longer than twenty-one days. My father set about convincing the Division of Military Applications in Washington, D.C., that a program under which Chinese scientists could come to Los Alamos to conduct research possessed tremendous potential benefits in terms of confidence-building between us and the Chinese. Furthermore, there would be no security risk if the visitors worked in non-classified areas. The policy was changed, and since that time a number of Chinese scientists have spent one to two years at Los Alamos working at LAMPF. The program has never resulted in any security problems.

Over the years, I have accompanied my father on several tours of the Meson Facility. He has a remarkable ability to explain very complex subjects in a way that a lay person can comprehend. I have been told by many who have worked with, and for, my father that he is one of the best-liked people at Los Alamos. They say this is because he always does his best to do the right thing, you can take him at his word, and he genuinely cares about the welfare of his employees as well as that of LANL.

After my father retired from LAMPF in 1985, he established the Center for National Security Studies at Los Alamos. The purpose of the center was to find ways to enhance international stability to reduce the risk of nuclear conflagration. Funding was granted, and he worked with the center until he retired in 1991. In summary, my father has devoted considerable effort and made substantial contributions toward fostering world peace. He is now one of six or eight "senior fellows" of LANL. This is the highest honor the lab can bestow upon someone. The board of regents of the University of California subsequently endowed him with the title of "Senior Fellow Emeritus."

I am extremely proud of my father for his many achievements. He has compiled an impressive list of awards and honors, the most significant of which are the E. O. Lawrence Award and a Guggenheim Fellowship.[8] He has also been nominated for the Fermi Award more than once. He would have been a hard act to follow had I gone into physics. He is mentioned in many who's whos, and even I am mentioned in *Who's Who in America*, where it says, "Son, Terry."

Of course, my father did make some very human mistakes. More than a few times he ended up driving the wrong way on a one-way street with four or more lanes of traffic bearing down on us. Ask him to drive around the block alone and he may get lost. Then there was the party for my sixth birthday. My mother took me and five friends to the one movie theater in town. She dropped us off and my father picked us up afterward. One kid didn't really want to come with us, but my father insisted. When we got home, my mother noticed there was one too many kids at the party. Fortunately, the "abductee's" mother was soon located, and she allowed him to stay for the rest of the party.

I found my father to be wrong about issues of significance only twice. The first was when I was seven. I had been given a book on rockets for Christmas, and I read it over and over. The book said that, in order to escape the earth's atmosphere, a rocket would have to accelerate at a rate of seven feet per second per second (not a typo)—an "impossible" feat. I asked my dad why it was impossible. He explained that the fuel required to achieve and maintain that rate of acceleration would be too heavy. I said, "But what if they had two or three parts on the rocket containing fuel which could be dropped off after the fuel had been used up?" He said, "The additional weight of the fuel and the increased size of the rocket would prevent that from working." About ten years later, following the launch of Sputnik, I reminded him of his error. He didn't recall it.

The other error occurred in 1985. As director of Denver's Office of Citizen Response, I was a mayoral appointee. Consequently, when Mayor McNichols lost his bid for reelection in 1983, I had to submit my resignation to the new mayor. After a few months the new mayor accepted my resignation, and while I was looking for a new job, my father suggested that I contact "Rocky Flats"—a nuclear weapons facility near Denver—regarding a position in public relations. For years, Rocky Flats had suffered from negative press, increasingly negative public opinion, and an endless string of public relations debacles due, in large part, to their dishonesty in their communications with the government and with the public. I said I doubted that Rocky Flats would be operating for much longer. My dad said, "Oh, no, no matter what happens, Rocky Flats will be making nuclear triggers for a long time to come." Although I made a couple of calls, I did not make a concerted effort to land a position there. A few years later, Rocky Flats ceased operations. If only *I* could say I had been wrong about only two things in my life.

Subsequent to my going to college, my dad has been supportive and has assisted me in my endeavors in myriad ways. Thus, I would say he has been a good father; but when I was a child his fathering was somewhat lacking, primarily because he was never there. Given the import of his work, the situation could not have been mitigated prior to the development of the H-bomb in 1952, except, perhaps, for the period from September 1945, with the end of the war, to September 1949, when the Soviets detonated their first atomic bomb. However, I feel that subsequent to 1952 he could have rearranged his priorities somewhat. By then, though, his work habits were well entrenched, and I don't think it ever occurred to him that there was a need to change. This was a state of affairs shared by most of the children of Los Alamos scientists of that era.

While attending the University of Alabama, my mother worked for Mr. Olan Mills in his new portrait photography business. She also did artwork for others on a contract basis and a lot of interior decorating and landscaping for friends and acquaintances. When LAMPF was built, she undertook to landscape the grounds of the facility.

In 1946, building began on the second permanent housing in Los Alamos—the "Western Area." My mother was chairperson of the three-member Housing Advisory Committee, on which Lois Bradbury also served. The committee was involved in decisions on design, landscaping, paint colors, and so forth. The committee got approval for a number of design changes that made the houses more habitable, such as adding fireplaces. When the first houses were painted, the builder mislaid the color key the committee had established, so the painting was done with whatever paint was available. The committee members were understandably incensed, and the builder was made to repaint the houses using the colors the committee had selected.

My mother was a multitalented artist. Painting was her forte, but the list of the various artistic talents at which she excelled is a lengthy one. She once wove a surreal underwater scene on some draperies and created a mosaic tabletop and other items in the same motif. Parts of that array were on view for many years at Santa Fe's Wheelwright Museum. She also has had other artworks displayed in museums, and her paintings have been displayed in several venues, including the Cherry Creek National Bank in Denver.

My mother was the consummate hostess. She maintained an immaculate household, did the taxes, and kept track of the money. My father's associates and/or my mother's friends frequently would stop by to visit, and she always made time for them. My father was usually late getting home from work, often bringing other people home for dinner with him with little or no notice, and she always accommodated the situation. She could put on a party for sixty people and make it look "as easy as pie." Then there was the constant stream of my friends in and out of the house. She always welcomed them and treated them as her own.

There was never a time when my mother wasn't heavily involved in the community, organizing arts and crafts classes, helping to found the Los Alamos chapter of the League of Women Voters, participating in chorale, and countless other activities. At the same time, she was always there for me—making Halloween costumes, baking cookies for Cub Scouts, helping my teachers with school projects, allowing me to use twenty or thirty decks of cards to build multistory card houses all over the living room, and not killing me for all the messes I made.

My mother relished helping visitors find temporary housing, taking them sightseeing and hosting parties for them. Her contagious good humor and helpfulness were a comfort to visitors and were widely recognized as a treasured asset of the lab. Sig Hecker, director of LANL from 1987 to 1998, once referred to her at a public ceremony as "the First Lady of LAMPF." In short, my mother influenced considerably the evolution of the community of Los Alamos.

– 5 –
Hiroshima!

It was years after the war before it was revealed to my parents' families that my father had worked on the Manhattan Project. We then learned that one of my mother's brothers, Tim Terry, had been on one of the two B-29s that followed the *Enola Gay*—the plane that dropped the atomic bomb on Hiroshima—to take photos of the damage.

In late 2000, after I had completed a first draft of this book, I encountered a lady whom I had dated around 1970 but hadn't seen for many years. She mentioned that she had some reading materials about Los Alamos that I had given to her, and she returned them to me. One of those items, amazingly, was an issue of the *Santa Fe New Mexican* newspaper, dated June 25, 1970. It was a keepsake issue in which was reprinted the front page and other articles that were first published on August 6, 1945, the day the A-bomb was dropped on Hiroshima. Following are excerpts from those articles.

Imagine that it is August 1945 and that you're learning about the atomic bomb for the first time. There is no commercial TV, so you have to rely on the radio and the newspaper for your information. We have been at war for nearly four years, and much of the world has been at war for far longer. Casualties from the war total in the tens of millions. Then, one morning, you read this:

Los Alamos Secret Disclosed by Truman[1]
ATOM BOMBS DROP ON JAPAN
Deadliest Weapons in World's History Made in Santa Fe Vicinity
Santa Fe learned officially today of a city of 6,000
in its own front yard.

The reverberating announcement of the Los Alamos bomb, with 2,000 times the power of the great Grand-Slammers dropped on Germany, also lifted the secret of the community on the Pajarito Plateau, whose presence Santa Fe has ignored, except in whispers, for more than two years.

Decision to locate the Atomic Bomb Project Laboratory on mesa an hour's drive from Santa Fe, meant that it was necessary for the Army Engineers to construct an entirely new town to house the workers and their families. Primary reason for selection of the isolated site was security.

Ranch School Site

When the army took over the property early in 1943 there were a few buildings which had been occupied by the Los Alamos Ranch School. New buildings began going up at once. Today there are 37 in the main technical area and about 200 others on the property used for the project itself. Three hundred buildings containing 620 family units also were constructed, as well as military barracks, hospital buildings and structures for administrative offices.

Dr. J. R. Oppenheimer, one of the foremost physicists in the country and director of the laboratory, came to the site during early stages of construction. Other scientists and technical workers followed soon after.

Scientific groups which had been working on the project elsewhere in the country moved in rapidly, bringing their equipment with them. The Harvard cyclotron was in operation six weeks after it had reached the site.

Tortuous Route

Nearest railroad facilities are at Albuquerque and Santa Fe. This made it necessary to truck everything from those cities, at least. The road from Santa Fe is a tortuous one, and in the beginning, the last 18 miles were not paved. This was bad enough for passenger cars and presented a particularly tough problem in hauling heavy loads.

Today the community has more than 6,000 residents. Slightly less than two-thirds are civilian men, women and children and the remainder military personnel. The post commander is Col. Gerald R. Tyler . . .

REVOLUTIONARY

News of the development at Los Alamos of the atomic bomb immediately raised conjecture regarding the potential industrial uses of the energy.

The power of the atomic force harnessed by scientists in the secret projects is almost beyond comprehension—one bomb packing the wallop of the bomb loads of 2,000 Superforts [B-29 bombers]. Talk was at once heard of the possibility of the newly controlled energy replacing coal, electricity, gasoline, water as a source of power.

That the study of the subject will continue was assured by the appointment by the Secretary of War of a committee to carry on investigation of atomic energy.

Spokesmen for the Los Alamos project said they had not been informed if this meant post-war continuation of the mountain project.

Now They Can Be Told Aloud, Those Stoories [sic] of "the Hill"

The secret of Los Alamos is out and the New Mexican staff and other news-papermen through New Mexico can heave a sigh—sigh, nothing; it's more of a groan—of relief.

President Truman's revelation today that it was an atomic bomb THEY were working on on the Hill ended what was probably the strictest censorship ever imposed upon the press of this state. There was practically no limit to the lengths that the guards went to and the situation at times became fantastically involved . . .

Notwithstanding the censorship, the news of Los Alamos had scarcely raced about the Plaza this morning when the membership of the "I Knew It All Along" club began growing by leaps and bounds. As a matter of record, the most recent rumor, No. 6892—straight from the horse's mouth last week—was that Alamos was working lickety-split night and day, in the production of windshield wipers for submarines.

The taboo on the mention of Los Alamos was final, complete and until today, irrevocable and not susceptible to any exceptions whatsoever.

A whole social world existed in nowhere in which people were married and babies were born nowhere. People died in a vacuum, autos and trucks crashed in a vacuum and the MPs baseball team materialized out of a vacuum . . . Even the graduates of Los Alamos Ranch School, the institution which preceded Uncle Sam's Atomic Bomb Project Laboratory, ceased to be graduates of Los Alamos; They bounded direct from Public School No. 7 clear into the classrooms of Harvard and Yale.

And on days when the Alamos experimenters threw their atomic bombs about a little too vigorously, and the windows of Santa Fe rattled ominously, this paper's phones would ring but the whole staff could just "no speak English."

The chain of secrecy about the project was maintained from the big cities in [the] East where workers were recruited clear through to the delivery of these same workers on The Hill. The Alamos bus stop was at Sena Plaza and people, laden with luggage and youngsters clinging in their arms, frequently barged into offices of that Plaza and inquired, "Where do we go to work?" One of the earliest bits of Alamos lore was that of the dude Wac who had never been farther west than Albany, N.Y.; she chose the moment when The Hill bus was turning the highest point on the Jemez mountains to peek out—and fainted dead away.

Under these conditions of secrecy rumors multiplied like maggots in ... garbage cans. Gas warfare, rockets, jet propulsion, death rays and—atomic bombs—were among the guesses most frequently voiced. During the last presidential campaign, Alamos—no foolin'—was sometimes [thought to be] a Republican internment camp.

In the early days of the project, even the "outside employees" who knew no more of what was going on than the Japs in the foxholes of Guadalcanal, were sworn never to reveal what they didn't know anyway, for the rest of their lifetime. Our own B.B. Dunne got tangled in the wringer for ... mentioning that "there were a lot of scientists in town."

Then there was the time that the New York Daily was whipping up a Sunday feature on Nobel Prize winners in the U.S. It queried The New Mexican for a brief summary of what Prof. X was doing now. The staff recognized the Alamos postoffice [*sic*] box number—that famous postal box where babies were born and to which whole crateloads of furniture were assigned—but it was decided to give the professor a whirl anyway on the old "You can't shoot me for trying" principle. A letter went out to Professor X in which an interview was asked.

The next morning at 8:09—their watches must have been slow—two guards jumped the cityroom. After a heap of protestations and avowals of innocence, it was agreed that the following telegram could be sent the News:

"Your man working for Mr. Whiskers on extremely hush-hush project. No Soap."

The telegram was delivered in New York by a Western Union boy flanked by a covey of guards. These men then began spilling all over the News cityroom like oranges out of a busted crate.

How, they wanted to know, did the News staff explain such Dick Tracy huggermugger stuff?

The News' difficulty was that the girl who had sent the telegram had gone on vacation and couldn't be reached. The News explained it after two clouded weeks in which, by report, you couldn't toss a cigarette in a wastepaper basket without setting fire to a guard.

The tantalizing little that Santa Feans knew about The Hill only heightened their interest. There were the lights to be seen from miles away; there were the days when fires raged and smoke billowed in the mountains and always the mysterious explosions ...[3]

'Utter Destruction,' Promised in Potsdam Ultimatum, Unleashed; Power Equals 2,000 Superforts

WASHINGTON, Aug. 6 (AP)—The U.S. Army Air Force has released on the Japanese an atomic bomb containing more power than 20,000 tons of TNT.

It produces more than 2,000 times the blast of the largest bomb ever used before.

The announcement of the development was made in a statement by President Truman released by the White House today.

The bomb was dropped 16 hours ago on Hiroshima, an important Japanese army base.

The President said that the bomb has "added a new and revolutionary increase in destruction" on the Japanese.

Mr. Truman added: "It is an atomic bomb. It is a harnessing of the basic power of the universe. The force from which the sun draws its power has been loosed against those who brought war to the Far East."

The base that was hit is a major quartermaster depot and has large ordnance, machine tool and air craft plants.

The raid on Hiroshima, located on Honshu Island on the shores of the Inland Sea, had not been disclosed previously although the 20th Air Force on Guam announced that 580 Superforts raided four Japanese cities at about the same time.

The city of 318,000 also contains a principal port.

2 Billion Gamble

The President disclosed that the Germans "worked feverishly" in search of a way to use atomic energy in their war effort but failed. Meantime American and British scientists studied the problem and developed two principal plants and some lesser factories for the production of atomic power.

The President disclosed that . . . "We have spent $2,000,000,000 on the greatest scientific gamble in history—and won."

"We are now prepared to obliterate more rapidly and completely every productive enterprise the Japanese have above ground in any city. We shall completely destroy Japan's power to make war."

The President noted that the Big Three ultimatum issued July 26 at Potsdam was intended "to spare the Japanese people from utter destruction" and the Japanese leaders rejected it. The atomic bomb now is the answer to that rejection and . . . "they may expect a rain of ruin from the air, the like of which has never been seen on this earth."

Process Secret

Mr. Truman forecast sea and land forces will follow up this air attack in such numbers and power as the Japanese never have witnessed.

The President said that this discovery may open the war for an entirely new concept of force and power. The actual harnessing of atomic energy may in the future supply the power that now comes from coal, oil and the great dams, he said.

"It has never been the habit of the scientists of this country or the policy of this government to withhold from the world scientific knowledge," Mr. Truman said. "Normally therefore everything about the work with atomic energy would be made public. That will have to wait, however, he said, until the war emergency is over.

MADE IN SANTA FE

WASHINGTON, Aug. 6 (AP)—The atomic bomb disclosed by President Truman today was developed at factories in Tennessee, Washington and New Mexico.

Mr. Truman said that from 65,000 to 125,000 workers were employed on the project at Oak Ridge near Knoxville, Tennessee, at I. . hland[4] [*sic*] near Pasco, Wash., and at an unnamed installation near Santa Fe, New Mexico.

He said the work was so secret that most of the employees did not know the character of it.

WILL SHORTEN WAR

WASHINGTON, Aug. 6 (AP)—Secretary Stimson predicted today that the atomic bomb will "prove a tremendous aid" in shortening the war with Japan.

The war secretary made his statement as the Army reported than an "impenetrable cloud of dust and smoke" cloaked Hiroshima after it was hit by the new weapon from the air.

An accurate assessment of the damage inflicted by the bomb is not yet available, however, the War Department said . . .

LONDON, Aug. 6 (AP)—Germany possessed some atomic power secrets, Winston Churchill said tonight, but "by God's mercy, British and American science outpaced all German efforts."

May Be Tool To End Wars; New Era Seen

Mankind's successful transition to a new age, the atomic age, was ushered in July 16, 1945 before the eyes of a tense group of renowned scientists and military men gathered in the desertlands of New Mexico to witness the first hand results of their $2,000,000,000 effort. Here in a remote section of the Alamogordo Air Base 120 miles southeast of Albuquerque the first man-made atomic explosion, the outstanding achievement of nuclear science, was achieved at 5:30 A.M. of that day.

Mounted on a steel tower, a revolutionary [weapon] destined to change war as it has been known [and] which [may well] be the instrumentality to end all wars, was set off with an impact which signalized man's entrance into a new physical world. Success was greater than the most ambitious estimates. A small amount of matter, the product of a chain of huge specially constructed industrial plants, was made to release the energy of the universe locked up within the atom from the beginning of time.

Credit J. R. Oppenheimer

This phase of the atomic bomb project, which is headed by Maj. Gen. Leslie R. Groves, was under the direction of Dr. J. R. Oppenheimer, theoretical physicist of the University of California. He is to be credited with achieving the implementation of atomic energy for military purposes.

Tension before the actual detonation was at a tremendous pitch. Failure was an ever-present possibility. Too great a success, envisioned by some of those present, might have meant an uncontrollable, unusable weapon.

Final assembly of the atomic bomb began on the night of July 12 in an old ranch house. As various component assemblies arrived from distant points, tension among the scientists rose to an increasing pitch. Coolest of all was the man charged with the actual assembly of the vital core, Dr. R. F. Bacher, in normal times a professor at Cornell University.

Lightning Threatens

On Saturday, July 14, the unit which was to determine the success or failure of the entire project was elevated to the top of the steel tower.

The ominous weather which had dogged the assembly of the bomb had a very sobering effect on the assembled experts whose work was accomplished amid lightening flashes and peals of thunder.

Nearest observation point was set up 10,000 yards south of the tower where in a timber and earth shelter the controls for the tests were located. At a point 17,000 yards from the tower at a point which would give the best observation the key figures in the atomic bomb project took their posts. These included General Groves, Dr. Vannevar Bush, head of the Office of Scientific Research and Development, and Dr. James B. Conant, president of Harvard University.

Lie Face Down

Actual detonation was in charge of Dr. K. T. Bainbridge of Massachusetts Institute of Technology. He and Lieutenant Bush, in charge of the Military Police Detachment, were the last men to inspect the tower with its cosmic bomb.

At the base camp, all present were ordered to lie on the ground, face downward, heads away from the blast direction.

Tension reached a tremendous pitch in the control room as the deadline approached. The several observation points in the area were tied in to the control room by radio . . .[5]

Another story in the same issue of the newspaper, although obviously written much later, tells about the early history of Los Alamos and expands upon what I have said about the inconveniences of the early years.

The fate of the Pajarito Plateau was sealed on November 25, 1942, in an Army memo to the Commanding General of Services of Supply. "There is a military necessity for the acquisition of this land" at Los Alamos, New Mexico, the memo said, for use as a "demolition range." The site included "approximately 54,000 acres" of which all but 8900 acres was public land supervised by the Forest Service. The Army estimated the cost of acquisition would be approximately $440,000 . . .

By the time the school had been notified nearly two weeks later, it had already become clear that the original estimated Project requirement of 30 scientists was illconsidered [sic] and that the Ranch School's 27 houses would be far from adequate. Therefore in December, when construction contracts were let, they included, in addition to laboratory buildings, temporary living quarters for a population of about 300 people. But even before the Ranch School students had left the Hill, construction crews had swelled the population to 1500.

On January 1, 1943, the University of California was selected to operate the new Laboratory and a formal nonprofit contract was soon drawn with the Manhattan Engineer District of the Army. By early spring, major pieces of borrowed equipment were being installed and a group of some of the finest scientific minds in the world were beginning to assemble on the Hill . . .

Recruiting was extremely difficult. Most prospective employees were already doing important work and needed good reason to change jobs, but because of the tight security regulations, only scientific personnel could be told anything of the nature of the work to be done. These scientists were able to recognize the significance of the project and be fascinated by the challenge. The administrative people and technicians, on the other hand, were expected to accept jobs in an unknown place for an unknown purpose. Not even wives could be told where the work would take them or why.

"The notion of disappearing into the desert for an indeterminate period and under quasi-military auspices disturbed a good many scientists and the families of many more," Oppenheimer recalled later.

The wife of one of the first scientists at the Project has written: "I felt akin to the pioneer women accompanying their husbands across uncharted plains westward, alert to dangers, resigned to the fact that they journeyed, for weal or woe, into the Unknown."

But journey they did, and throughout the spring and summer of 1943 hundreds of bewildered families converged on New Mexico to begin their unforgettable adventure.

The first stop for new arrivals—civilian and military alike—was the Project's Santa Fe Office at 109 East Palace Avenue. There, under the portal of one of the oldest buildings in Santa Fe, newcomers received a warm welcome from Dorothy McKibbin who was to manage the office for twenty years.

"They arrived, those souls in transit, breathless, sleepless, haggard and tired," Mrs. McKibbin has written. "Most of the new arrivals were tense with expectancy and curiosity. They had left physics, chemistry or metallurgical laboratories, had sold their homes or rented them, had deceived their friends and launched forth to an unpredictable world."

As their first contact with that unpredictable world, Mrs. McKibbin soothed nerves, calmed fears and softened disappointments. She also supervised shipment of their belongings, issued temporary passes and arranged for their transportation up the hill to Los Alamos.

At the end of the tortuous, winding dirt road, the newcomers found a remarkable city. They found a ramshackle town of temporary buildings scattered helter-skelter over the landscape, an Army post that looked more like a frontier mining camp.

"It was difficult to locate any place on that sprawling mesa which had grown so rapidly and so haphazardly, without order or plan," wrote one early arrival.

Haste and expediency, under the urgency of war, guided every task. Equipment and supplies were trucked from the railhead at Santa Fe while temporary wooden buildings were being hastily thrown together to house them. Streets for the town and roads to remote sites were appearing daily under the blades of countless bulldozers.

... Ranch School buildings ... had been converted for Project use. Fuller Lodge had become a restaurant, the classrooms ... converted to a Post Exchange and other shops. The masters' houses had become residences for top Project administrators. As the only houses in Los Alamos offering tubs instead of showers, this group of buildings quickly became known as "Bathtub Row," a name that has stuck to this day.

The hurriedly built, green Laboratory buildings sprawled along the south side of Ashley Pond. Rows of four-family apartment houses spread to the west along Trinity Drive and northward; rows of barracks and dormitories bordered the apartments and overlooked horse pastures which are now the Western Area. East of

Ashley Pond spread the less luxurious housing including the sections known as McKeeville and Morganville.

The Army did its best to find a place for everyone. Even as the incoming population was spilling over into neighboring valley ranches, to Frijoles Lodge at Bandelier and to Santa Fe, night shift workers, maintenance crews and specialists imported from far away were pouring onto the mesa to be sandwiched in somewhere. The four-family Sundt apartments and the McKee houses were built and occupied at a frantic pace with Pacific hutments, government trailers, expansible trailers and prefabricated units following in jerry-built procession. For more than 20 years the housing never quite managed to catch up with the demand.

This unsightly assortment of accommodations ranged row on row along unpaved and nameless streets. A forest of tall metal chimneys for coal, wood and oil burning stoves pierced the air. Soot from furnaces and dust from the streets fell in endless layers on every surface. Winter snows and summer rains left streets and yards mired in mud.

There was only one telephone line (furnished by the Forest Service) when 1943 began and only three until 1945. Dry cleaning had to be sent to Santa Fe until the establishment of a laundry and cleaning concession in the summer of 1944. The first resident dentist arrived in 1944 and a Project hospital was established the same year.

There was never enough water. Dr. Walter Cook, who organized the school system in 1943 remembers the wooden water tank that stood near Fuller Lodge.

"It had a guage [*sic*] on the outside that indicated the water level," said Dr. Cook. "It was the only way we could tell when we could take a bath."

But life in Los Alamos was not entirely primitive. A 12-grade school system with 16 teachers was established in 1943. A town council was formed the same year. Its members elected by popular vote to serve as an advisory committee to the community administration. A nursery school was established for working mothers and a maid service, using Indian women from nearby pueblos, was provided on a rationing system based upon the number and ages of the woman's children and the number of hours she worked.

More than 30 recreational and cultural organizations were formed during the army years and in 1945 a group, including Enrico Fermi and Hans Bethe, founded a loosely knit Los Alamos University which provided lectures and published lecture notes in fields of nuclear physics and chemistry. Credits from these courses were accepted by leading universities across the country. Home grown talent provided concerts and theatrics and there were movies several times a week. And there was the country. Los Alamos, for all its ugliness, was surrounded by some of the most spectacular scenery in America.

"Whenever things went wrong, and that was often," one resident said, "we always had our mountains—the Jemez on one side, the Sangre de Cristos on the other."

But Los Alamos was also surrounded by a high barbed wire fence and armed guards. In what was probably the most secret project the United States has ever had, secrecy became a way of life. Laboratory members were not allowed personal contact with relatives nor permitted to travel more than 100[6] miles from Los Alamos. A chance encounter with a friend outside the Project had to be reported in detail to the security force.

Anonymity prevailed. Famous names were disguised and occupations were not mentioned ... The word physicist was forbidden; everyone was an "engineer." Driver's licenses, auto registrations, bank accounts, income tax returns, food and gasoline rations and insurance policies were issued to numbers. Out going mail was censored and long distance calls were monitored. No one was permitted to mention names or occupations of fellow residents, to give distances or names of nearby places or even to describe a beautiful view lest the location be pinpointed. Incoming mail was addressed simply to "P.O. Box 1663, Santa Fe, New Mexico," an obscurity that cloaked the existence of Los Alamos during the entire war.

Recalls one early resident, "I couldn't write a letter without seeing a censor poring over it. I couldn't go to Santa Fe without being aware of hidden eyes upon me, watching, waiting to pounce on that inevitable misstep. It wasn't a pleasant feeling."

Tight security regulations plagued scientific progress, too. The military insisted that individual scientific projects be strictly compartmentalized and not discussed so that no one could see the overall progress—or purpose—of the mission. But Director Oppenheimer, knowing that cross-fertilization of ideas among scientists is infinitely useful in solving problems, balked and as a result weekly colloquia were begun and continue in Los Alamos today. Because of such major victories as this over military rigidity, Oppenheimer is credited not only with the success of the Project but the high morale that made it possible.

The Army years at Los Alamos were a time of chaos and achievement, of unaccustomed hardship and exhausting work. But, as Oppenheimer was to report later, "Almost everyone knew that this job, if it were achieved, would be part of history. This sense of excitement, of devotion and of patriotism in the end prevailed."[7]

Yet another article discussed in detail the events leading up to the Trinity test. At one point it stated: "the nagging uncertainty persisted about whether the bomb would work at all." It continued:

Then, as if things weren't dismal enough, a meeting of Trinity people held just before the test heard Hans Bethe describe in depressing detail all that was known about the bomb, and all that wasn't. Physicist Frederic Reines remembers the utter dejection he felt after hearing the report. "It seemed as though we didn't know anything," he said.[8]

Note that the headline said "Bombs," while, in fact, it was a single bomb. The headline writer probably couldn't fathom that a large city had been destroyed by a single bomb. Also, it is remarkable to me, given that Project Y remained the "Secret City" for a number of years following Hiroshima, that the *New Mexican* was allowed to release as much information as they were on August 6, 1945.

One argument in favor of using the atomic bomb in World War II that I have never seen mentioned in a textbook is that, after the Trinity test, we had only two bombs left. If one were used for a demonstration, as Leo Szilard and others proposed, we would have had just one left. At the same time, giving the impression that we had an unlimited supply was considered to be a significant factor in trying to convince the Japanese to surrender quickly, and it would have taken weeks or months to assemble additional bombs. I have also heard that some Japanese were thankful that the atomic bomb was used because they believe that, without something of that shock value, the military leaders of Japan would have resisted to the point of the obliteration of their entire civilization.[9]

In addition to the usual arguments for having used the bomb, such as the hundreds of thousands, if not millions, of American and Japanese lives saved, I believe there was a major unintended benefit derived from its use against Hiroshima and Nagasaki. It may well have contributed to the fact that the bomb has not been used since, because the horror that is the atomic bomb became a reality. Most of us have seen pictures of the death and destruction reaped by the bomb. Lacking that, I believe some countries, including the United States, might have been more tempted to use it in subsequent conflagrations. Had that occurred, its use might have resulted in even graver consequences, and without the offsetting benefit of saving innumerable American and Japanese lives by eliminating the need for the United States to invade Japan.

What if the public had remained unaware of the potential devastation of nuclear weapons until the USSR and the United States had vast stockpiles of such bombs? There might never have been a public outcry to "ban the bomb" with which to temper military aspirations and guide government decision-making. Thus, public opinion might well have played a lesser role in deterring war between the major world powers subsequent to 1945. Perhaps we should be thankful that the bomb was used when there were only two of them to use.

6

What? No Oscar?

I have no recollection of the Trinity test, although the detonation could be seen and heard from Los Alamos. Of course, I was only eighteen months old. Seth Neddermeyer, still smarting from having been removed by Oppie as leader of the group working on implosion, refused to go to the site for the test. Instead, he went up to the Valle Grande with a number of other scientists and watched from there—180 miles from ground zero.

My father also took my mother and me up there to see it. However, because detonation was postponed until 5:30 A.M., and since my father couldn't tell my mother what it was they were supposed to see, my mother insisted he take us home before "it" happened. I suspect she was concerned about me; it gets pretty chilly at night in the Valle, even in July. Furthermore, I don't think they missed much, because it was overcast that night. Thus, unlike those who ventured down to Chupadero Peak, if anyone in the Valle Grande saw anything at all, it was probably nothing more than a brightening of the clouds in the southern sky.

In some ways, of course, growing up in Los Alamos was similar to growing up in any small town, but in many ways it was truly unique! A fence encircled the entire community. On the east, it was a high-security fence. On the west and north sides, where the mountains rose rather steeply, it was mostly just "run-of-the-mill" four-foot-high barbed wire fence with frequent signs stating, "Government Property, Keep Out." There was essentially no crime, and there were no strangers of whom to be fearful. That may be why I have always tended to be more trusting, open, and outgoing toward others than are most people. The only thefts of which I am aware were those perpetrated by the ravens that stole golf balls by the hundreds on the golf course.

In the early days there was very little traffic, because most people lived within walking distance of their jobs and few had cars (or gas). Some of the émigré scientists found the surrounding fence disturbing because it reminded them of the German concentration camps; however, as a child, I never felt it limited my freedom of movement. If anything, I perceived the fence as security from the outside world, but what did I know of concentration camps?

As a child I was not particularly concerned about the fact that there were no stores in which to shop other than the commissary. Most retail stores didn't do well in Los Alamos in the early days (and, indeed, I believe they still struggle today). Perhaps it was because going to Santa Fe was more than just an opportunity to go to a variety of stores to shop—it was a temporary escape, and well-established habits die hard.

Of course we kids didn't realize that our childhood was unusual. We didn't know that there was any other way to grow up. The fact that we had to participate in practice evacuations when the air raid sirens wailed wasn't unusual for the time. On the other hand, we were made well aware of the fact that what went on at the lab made us a prime target for the enemy (the USSR). We also knew that we might need to evacuate if something went wrong at the lab, but for us that was just the way it was.

From a young boy's perspective, Los Alamos was a great place! There were a lot of sports, including baseball, basketball, football, tennis, golf, skiing, skating, fishing, hunting, hiking, and camping. However, for adults who were not into sports or outdoor activities, entertainment options were severely limited. For a long time, there was just one restaurant, the "mess hall," a "Little Theater" group, a few arts and garden groups, and not much else. Nightlife was, and still is, pretty much nonexistent. Consequently, as an adult, I have always been averse to the idea of returning to Los Alamos to live.

My earliest clear recollection is that of following a deer up a path on my tricycle, less than a hundred yards from our new Western Area house. The deer was only six feet or so in front of me and totally ignored my presence. I followed it until my mom called me and said I was getting too far from home.

My next recollection is of a visit by my father's parents in the winter of 1947. Therefore, any information I provide on events prior to 1947 came from other sources. As their plane landed in Albuquerque, it twice bounced ten feet or more off the ground before landing hard. This was the first time I had ever seen airplanes land; however, we had been watching other planes land and none of them had bounced, so we were concerned that my grandparents might have been injured. Well, they said they were just fine, and since they had never flown before, they assumed it was a normal landing. However, when it came time to go back to New York, they decided to take the train.

When we got back to Los Alamos with my grandparents, it was cold and snowy. One day while they were there, I played hide and seek in the house with my grandpa. I crawled under my mom's sewing desk and pulled the chair in after me. My grandpa couldn't find me and I fell asleep. Before I woke, everyone became concerned that I might have gone outside, so they called the police. I awakened, heard a commotion, climbed out of my hiding place, and said, "What's going on?" Boy, did everybody look surprised!

My earliest friend with whom I have maintained contact is David Carlson. We were close to the same age and extremely competitive, which led to endless squabbles. When we were about six months old, we were playing in the sandbox and David clobbered me over the head with a toy shovel. He still reminds me of it. Well, I got even with him! I wet the bed one night, and when confronted I said, "David Carlson did it." This in spite of the fact that the Carlsons had moved to Teseque, halfway between Los Alamos and Santa Fe (about twenty miles), and David hadn't been to our house for days.

After the travel restrictions were lifted, when my parents wanted to get away for a weekend, they often took me to stay with the Carlsons. Of course, when the Carlsons wanted to get away, my parents reciprocated and David stayed with us.

One time when I was staying with the Carlsons, David and I found a garden snake that had been injured by some sharp instrument. We captured it and put it in the bathtub with a little water, hoping we could somehow nurse it back to health. However, David's mother happened upon the snake while we were out in the yard playing, disposed of the poor thing, and then was irate with us when she learned that we put it there. Our intentions were so honorable, how could she be upset with us?

One day a couple of years later, the Rosens and the Carlsons were on a picnic near Los Alamos, and David and I found where a couple of snakes had shed their skins. We thought it was neat, so we ran back to tell our parents. When we got back, we immediately started telling about what we had seen. Before we finished the story, my dad said, "Don't anybody move or say anything!" He and David's dad, Bengt, picked up some large rocks and hurled them at a spot about four feet behind my mother. They had seen a rattler heading right for her and, fortunately, they got it before it got her. After they explained to us that it was a poisonous snake, David and I gave snakes a little wider berth.

By the time I was four or five, my dad sometimes took me to his lab after hours and on weekends when he had work to do. I loved it! The guard allowed me to go in with him—something even my mom couldn't do. His lab was adjacent to the old Ranch School icehouse, where all fissionable material was kept in the early days. Consequently, it was the most heavily guarded building in the whole laboratory. My father had about twenty women working for him in microscopy, and each of them had a microscope and a mechanical calculator.

I once asked my father why all of his employees were women. He explained that, due to the housing shortage in the early days, it was necessary to train the spouses of current lab employees to do this work. Furthermore, he said that due to the eyestrain of working with microscopes, no one was allowed to work with them for more than four hours a day, so his employees had to have some other source of income, such as a working spouse. In addition, he said that no men ever applied for the job.

My dad wouldn't let me play with the microscopes, but I spent hours playing with the calculators. The calculator keys were like those of an old manual typewriter, and if you struck two or more keys at the same time, they got stuck. I suspect that, by my efforts alone, Dick Feynman could have been kept busy for hours after each of my visits. However, in the several years before my father stopped taking me, I figured out how to fix all but the most stubborn jams myself.

There were no hotels or motels in early Los Alamos, and a lot of visitors stayed with us in the 1940s and 1950s. Whenever that happened, I was routinely transferred from my bedroom to the smaller spare bedroom that doubled as my mother's sewing room. Ken Erikson was the second physics student to do his graduate work under the tutelage of my father, and we became close friends with Ken and his wife, Jewell. After Ken completed his doctorate, the Eriksons moved to Albuquerque, but they frequently came to Los Alamos for the weekend. On one such occasion, when I was about four, Jewell was in our only bathroom and I needed to tinkle. I didn't like locked doors and already had learned how to "jimmy" all of the locks in the house. I knocked on the door and told Jewell I needed to come in. Jewell said, "I'm taking a shower and the door is locked." I said, "That's okay, I have my own key." So I unlocked the door, went in, and tinkled. Jewell was speechless, as well as clothesless. What is really surprising to me is that, despite all of their tribulations with me, the Eriksons later adopted two children of their own.

Just before I started kindergarten, my parents took me to Denver for the first time. Shortly after we arrived, I was standing outside the motel and suddenly started jumping up and down and screaming, "Look! A real live charlie (trolley) car!" One of my favorite books was about a trolley, but I had no idea such things actually existed. I got so excited, my parents decided we needed to do more traveling so I would get to know the "real world." Thereafter, we went to Colorado almost every year, just before school started.

In the late 1940s, when children were exposed to a disease, they were isolated, or "quarantined," for two weeks or so to avoid exposing others. As a first-grader I was quarantined for seventy-five days for chicken pox. I occupied my time at home taking on the characteristics of one animal or another. One time, I behaved like a squirrel, eating nuts while perched on a windowsill. The next time I was a fox, a bear, or a deer. I became so engrossed in my adopted "beings" that my parents were somewhat concerned for my mental health. Consequently, they reported to the health authorities that I had contracted a mild case of chicken pox so I could stay in school. Despite the fact that there were no inoculations available, I never caught the chicken pox or any of the other childhood diseases. I have since regretted that because of my children and, more recently, my grandchildren, due to the possibility they might bring these things home from school with them.

Soon after I entered the first grade I met someone who became my closest friend throughout life. There was a hiatus of ten or twelve years due to "spiritual" differences, but we have since become extremely close again. I never stopped considering him to be my brother, and I suspect that he would say the same. For months after we met, my mom would not allow me to bring my new friend home to play after school. However, once she learned that Terry Anna was a boy and not a girl (Terryanna), everything was okay.

Some months before I entered the first grade, Johnny Goldstein, a friend who lived across the street, introduced me to the game of chess. I told my dad that I really liked chess and wanted to get good at it. He told me that, to become a good chess player, one had to play at least five hundred games a year. Figuring that I might not have much time to play chess after school started, I set out to play more than five hundred games during the summer. I kept count of the number of games I played and far exceeded my target. Sure enough, I got to be pretty good! By the time I was seven, I was beating my father so badly that he wouldn't play me anymore.

We started learning to read in the first grade. The big innovation at the time was to teach kids how to read phonetically. I think it was fairly successful, but I also think it had a lot to do with the fact that I have always been a poor speller. I'll bet that the person who developed the spelling of the word *phonetically* had a great sense of humor.

It was at about this same time that our class walked across the street to the high school to see the original "Smoky the Bear." He had been rescued from a New Mexico forest fire and treated by a Santa Fe veterinarian, and he was still covered with bandages from his ordeal. While the rangers were telling us about Smoky, they taught us this song: *"Smoky the Bear, Smoky the Bear, a-growlin' and a-prowlin' and a-sniffin' the air. He can smell a fire before it starts to flame, that's why they call him Smoky, that is how he got his name."*[1]

Sometime later it occurred to me that the song was probably preaching an untruth. I figured that if Smoky could smell fire before it started to flame, he should have been able to escape the fire without getting burned.

I was five or six when I learned to ski and ice skate. My parents didn't ski, but lots of our friends did, and there was always someone willing to take me along for the ten-minute drive to Sawyer's Hill. The toughest part for me was getting on the tow rope, but after I mastered that, I enjoyed it so much that I always hated to leave. I got to be pretty good, but after high school, I just didn't want to commit the time and money necessary to continue. It just seemed like such an effort to have to drive for an hour or so to get to a ski area after having been spoiled by the convenience of Sawyer's Hill.

Ice skating was another story. I couldn't understand why I was having so much trouble learning to do it until someone explained that I had weak ankles. I went ice skating maybe twice a year and I never got beyond the beginner stage. I can't remember ever really enjoying it—I would just try to stay upright and moving until my feet froze solid. Then I'd waddle into the warming house to thaw them out.

The summer after the first grade, I undertook my first business endeavor. The Paxtons lived a few houses down from my parents. They had a daughter my age, and one day she sold something to my mom for a quarter. Not to be outdone, I stripped several sunflowers of their seeds and went up and down the street selling them five for a penny or something. Hugh's wife, Jean, very kindly purchased a quarter's worth of sunflower seeds. Although it was not my most profitable venture, it was far from my least successful. At least I didn't lose any money.

I also began coin collecting that summer. Whenever I could get my mother to take me to the bank, I spent an hour or so going through their pennies, nickels, and dimes. I bought five dollars' worth at a time, looked through them, repackaged them, and traded them in for another five dollars' worth. I did this until I had looked at every coin the bank had on hand that day, or so they said. After a few years, I started riding my bike the two miles or so to the bank several times a week for the same purpose. I'll bet they just loved to see me coming.

Coin collecting not only led to my second business endeavor—cataloging and selling my extra coins of value to collectors to other people—it led to my first moral dilemma. The coins all said, "In God We Trust." I didn't trust in God. I didn't even know the man. Although I had heard a lot of people talk about him, I wasn't at all sure there was such a person—kind of like Santa, except that I was pretty sure Santa existed. I mean, there was hard evidence. Every Christmas morning there were gifts under the tree that hadn't been there the night before, and the tags said they were from Santa. Furthermore, Santa never failed to consume the milk and cookies I left for him. I had never seen God do anything like that.

For fear of being ostracized, I didn't want to make a big deal out of the fact that I didn't "trust in God." Although I wasn't convinced that God existed, I wasn't sure. I thought that maybe it was one of those things you came to understand as you got older. Some years later, the clause "under God" was inserted in the Pledge of Allegiance, which we recited every day in school. I still didn't believe in God, and I felt dishonest saying "under God," so when we got to that part, I just didn't say those words. That was the only way I felt I could balance what I perceived to be the expectations of others with my desire not to be dishonest, but I was never comfortable with it.

Of course, I have since learned that I am not the only one who has doubts about the existence of God and that there is even a name for such people—agnostic. By my definition, agnostic means that I am absolutely, positively certain that God may, or may not, exist.

I also joined the Cub Scouts when I was six. We went on lots of hikes and overnight camping trips in the surrounding mountains, and we could earn "arrowheads" (cloth triangles that your mom always sewed on your Cub Scout shirt without too much urging) by doing various projects like learning the Morse Code.

Although I'm not sure either of us ever verbalized it, I competed with Johnny Goldstein to see who could earn the most arrowheads. I beat him by one—twenty to nineteen. That was the most arrowheads a Cub Scout had ever earned in Los Alamos. I was so proud of my achievement that I still have that shirt in the closet.

After I had earned the highest Cub Scout badge, the "Webelos," I looked at joining the Boy Scouts. I attended one meeting, but when they recited the Boy Scout pledge, it became apparent that they all professed to believe in God. I still had my doubts about God, so I didn't go back.

My agnostic leanings undoubtedly derived from my upbringing. My mother was raised Southern Methodist, but my father, despite his Jewish parents, has always been nonreligious. I believe that he would have said he was an atheist before he was involved in a serious auto accident in 1967, but he is now openly agnostic. I don't recall God or religion ever having been discussed in our house during my formative years.

Once in a while we would drive the hundred miles to Albuquerque. I never particularly enjoyed going, because it seemed so far away and so often it was uncomfortably hot—especially in the desert between Santa Fe and Albuquerque—and of course there was no air-conditioning in those days. It seemed like the wind was always blowing lots of dirt around in Albuquerque. It took long enough to get there that we usually had to stay the night, and my asthma (which I developed around age six) always tended to act up, probably because of all that blowing dirt.

It was terribly barren between Santa Fe and Bernalillo—a suburb of Albuquerque—and the only thing we ever saw was a number of little lean-to stalls where the Indians sold and traded their wares. They had handmade blankets, silver and turquoise jewelry, beaded items such as tiny moccasins and headbands, and even legs of lamb.

Occasionally we would trade a couple of old pairs of pants for a blanket or something. With the prices commanded by those craft items today, it's a shame that we didn't invest in more of them. The Indians also had some of those lean-tos between Española and Santa Fe, and I think that their primary ware was pottery. There were more lean-tos between Española and Taos, but I think they were maintained more by Hispanics than by Indians, and they sold primarily fruits and chili *ristras* (strings of chilies).

In early September every year, my folks and I would head for Santa Fe to go see one of the more spectacular and peculiar events there—the burning of Zozobra (Spanish for "anxiety")[2]. We would begin by having lunch at "The Shed" in Burro Alley, or at La Fonda Hotel. Then we'd run some always-needed errands; pick up some dry cleaning, go to Kaune's meat market, and so on. Then, in midafternoon, we'd head for a large park on the north end of town to see the burning of Zozobra. This was the kickoff event of the annual fiesta in Santa Fe.[3]

Zozobra was also known as "Old Man Grouch" and "Old Man Gloom." For many years I thought Zozobra derived from the melding of the area's Native American culture with that of the Conquistadors. However, I have since learned that Zozobra evolved from the mind of well-known Santa Fe artist Will Schuster in about 1924 as part of a lighthearted poke at the religious pomp and circumstance of the annual Santa Fe Fiesta. Others involved in the original effort included such well-known town characters as B.B. Dunne. B.B. was a longtime columnist for the *Santa Fe New Mexican* who, from the time I was old enough to recognize him, seemed to hang out interminably in the lobby of La Fonda.

The first time I remember seeing Zozobra I was absolutely awestruck! There were hundreds (now it's thousands) of people sitting on the tops of their cars. On a hill in front of us was this twenty-five- to thirty-foot-tall marionette that looked to me like a real live goblin. It was really kind of frightening, but my parents assured me that what was happening was okay—that the burning of Zozobra was supposed to send all our troubles up in flames so we could enter the new year trouble-free. That was an encouraging thought, but it always seemed strange that I didn't feel any different afterward.

As dusk crept toward darkness, some people in black hoods and robes approached Zozobra, and after some ceremonial mumbo jumbo that I remember only vaguely, they lit him on fire. Then they flung off their robes, and they and a number of other people began doing some strange and mysterious dance around him as the flames engulfed him. Zozobra moaned and groaned as though the flames really did hurt, and fireworks began spewing their glorious colors skyward. His moaning seemed to grow louder as the flames shot higher! His toothless mouth opened and closed, his arms flailed around, and his huge glowing eyes rolled in his head until, suddenly, he was gone and everyone cheered!

It seemed as though Zozobra grew a little bit taller and more sophisticated every year. I've been told that he was fifty feet tall in 2000. I haven't been to see him for years now, because I've been told that it's so crowded you can't get close enough for a good view unless you get there before noon. However, once you have seen

Zozobra, you never forget him. Many towns and cities with Hispanic populations—especially in Mexico—have fiestas, but Zozobra is unique to Santa Fe.

In order to get to Santa Fe or Albuquerque, we had to cross the old Otowi Bridge. The bridge was extremely narrow, and at the south end, the road turned sharply to curve around Buckman Mesa. There was a large stone stanchion on each side of each end of the bridge, and the ones on the south end had innumerable paint marks and scratches. One scientist's wife, Miriam Landshoff, had particularly great difficulty negotiating that turn onto the bridge, and her husband, Rolf, was forever coming to our house to borrow my father's sledgehammer (to pound the car fender back out). One Saturday my father needed his sledgehammer for something, so he walked to the Landshoffs' house to borrow it back. When he asked Rolf for the sledgehammer, Rolf said: "Can you wait until after five o'clock? Meriam went to Santa Fe today."

Christmastime was, like so many things in Los Alamos, somewhat unusual. Despite my lack of religious convictions, I have always enjoyed singing Christmas carols, and I heartily support the "Christmas spirit." We went to lots of Christmas parties, and my parents usually hosted one of the larger ones during the holidays. After John Allred married Elizabeth Bode (pronounced "Bodee") in 1951, we often went to Elizabeth's hometown of Abiquiu on Christmas eve. Abiquiu was a quaint little Hispanic village about thirty-five miles north of Los Alamos. Elizabeth had a lovely younger sister, Charlotte, and one Christmas Eve I unfortunately broke her heart when I told her that there was no Santa Claus. At the time, I didn't realize the hurt I had caused her, but she reminded me of it when I next saw her after a hiatus of about forty-five years.

As with much of northern New Mexico at Christmastime, many of the rooftops and adobe walls of Abiquiu were illuminated with rows of small paper bags weighed down with sand with candles in them (farolitos). We went to the Bodes' home for dinner, lit a bunch of bonfires (luminarias), and watched a candlelit procession wander through town. They were reenacting Joseph and Mary's search for a place to stay, and they finally ended up at the church in the town square. Then Elizabeth's family went to mass and we headed home to Los Alamos.

I had always been unsure about whether the candles in bags were *farolitos* or *luminarias*. I recently consulted with a number of people who have lived in New Mexico for over fifty years, and they are evenly divided in their opinions of which word refers to which item. A representative of the Santa Fe Chamber of Commerce says that *farolitos* are the bags with candles in them, and *luminarias* are the little bonfires. I got a confirmation of this from the retired owner of a gas station in Abiquiu, Elizabeth Allred's brother, Carl.

Georgia O'Keeffe's home/studio was in Abiquiu. Although many people didn't like her, and vice versa, she and my parents always got along well. I, however, found her very unpleasant, and my guess is that she didn't like me or any other kid. I found her to be exceedingly self-centered and always desirous of being the center of attention. My father describes her as behaving more queenlike than most queens. I loved her house, though, because it looked like a mysterious fortress from the outside. However, whenever we went inside, she never allowed me to look around. She always insisted that I sit, remain still, and not say anything. The only time I got to see anything was when I asked if I could go to the bathroom. I hated sitting still, so I usually "had to go" at least two or three times while we were there. Well, I got even by deciding I didn't like her artwork. I concede that it's not bad, but I still don't like it. I guess I showed her!

According to my father, Georgia had two outfits—black for winter and white for summer. Whenever her sister, Claudia, was planing to visit from back East, Claudia would call my mother and ask her to do some advance scouting to find hats for her to try on in the shops in Santa Fe.

I also knew "Maria the Potter" and Helen Cordero of Storyteller Doll fame. Maria was a delightful lady. She was the first to rediscover the lost art of producing black pottery. As I recall, it has something to do with smoking the pottery with burning cow dung. More than once, we went to San Ildefonso to see Indian dances and dined with her family afterward. I remember Helen only vaguely, but she and my mother were good friends for many years.

When I was about six, a film company came to film a western—

Four Flags West—at Edith Warner's house by the Otowi Bridge. It starred Joseph Cotton and Linda Darnell. I got to play the part of an Indian one day. I sat in a tree with a bow and arrow waiting to ambush a wagon train and they paid me five dollars just for sitting there. Better yet, Linda Darnell kissed me on the cheek. I never wanted to wash my face again. At one point, Linda came riding by on her galloping horse and pulled me onto the horse with her. They wanted to do it again for the film, but I would have had to miss some school, and my mom said no. I've been told that Burl Ives was also in that movie and that, at one point, he had me on his horse with him, too, but I don't remember it.

At the time of the filming, my parents and I, along with five or six other Los Alamos families, were helping Tilano build Edith Warner a new adobe house farther back from the road and the river. Tilano taught us how to make adobe bricks and *vigas*, or rough-hewn logs. When it was done it was a beautiful house with its fireplaces and ceilings with *vigas*. With her new, larger house, Edith was able to run a primitive but picturesque tearoom and restaurant. Thereafter, we were always welcome at the San Ildefonso and Santa Clara Pueblos. Many a time we went to see their dances—long before they allowed the public to view them—and went to the governor's house for a meal afterward. Also, despite the Indians' strong feelings at that time against allowing pictures to be taken of them or their ceremonies, they allowed my father to do so.

Tilano was wonderful to us kids. For Christmas, he made us bows and arrows and brought us lots of small bundles of wood with which to make *luminarias*. It was quite an experience growing up among the Indians with their ancient ways, while seeing the cutting edge of science evolving at Los Alamos, just ten miles away. There was something strangely incongruous about it, yet there it was.

7

From Hot to Cold (War)

As I have said previously, after the war ended, it was not at all clear whether Los Alamos would continue to exist. Lab employees had been on a six-day workweek during the war; it was reduced to five as soon as the war was over. Many of the scientists who had been professors at major universities or researchers in private industry returned to the positions they had held before the war. Even if the future of the lab had not been uncertain, many would have left, some because of the less-than-favorable living conditions, some for philosophical reasons, and others because they preferred the life of a professor to that of a researcher.

Many of the scientists, like my father, had come to Los Alamos right out of graduate school and had no pre-established career. When World War II came to an end, a lot of them began looking for jobs elsewhere, just in case the lab closed, but quite a few of them remained at Los Alamos throughout the transition to a post-war research facility. My father was among this latter group.

Given all the work with radioactive elements at Los Alamos, it amazes me that there have been only three fatalities related to nuclear materials over the years. The first was Harry Daghlian in 1945. He caused a mass of plutonium to go critical[1] for an instant, thereby releasing a lethal dose of radiation. Harry was alone at the time, so no one else was injured.

The second was Louis Slotin in 1946. He was performing a demonstration and was using a screwdriver to maintain separation between two hemispheres of beryllium surrounding the ball of plutonium mentioned above. The screwdriver slipped and the two halves of the beryllium casing closed. This caused the plutonium to go critical for a fraction of a second. Louis was able to get the two hemispheres apart again, but he had already received a lethal dose of radiation. Several other people in the room suffered lesser degrees of radiation poisoning, and after that, new rules were implemented mandating that all work with potential critical masses be done by remote control.

There was a bit of irony in these accidents because, according to Otto Frisch, the two individuals who gave him driving lessons were Harry Daghlian and, subsequently, Louis Slotin.[2] Could Otto have been such a bad driver that he drove his teachers to distraction? Who knows? The day after getting his license, Otto did run into a tree, knocking one of his passengers, Perce King, unconscious.

Although I did not know Louis Slotin, I did know several of the people who were in the room with him at the time. Al Graves, whom I knew fairly well, was standing closest to Louis when the accident occurred. Al received a substantial dose of radiation, and the fillings in his teeth became quite radioactive. His wife, Elizabeth, who was also a physicist, devised a shield of base metal to fit over his teeth so the radiation would not do further damage to his gums or cheeks. Al made a full recovery, as far as I know.

In 1958 there was one more fatality in what was termed a "plant accident." A technician by the name of Kelly was handling a container of plutonium in solution when it spontaneously went critical. Kelly was the only casualty.

Hugh Paxton earned his doctorate under the tutelage of physics Nobel Laureate (1939) E. O. Lawrence (1901–58) at Berkeley in 1937. He then spent a year helping the French chemistry Nobel Laureate (1935) Frédéric Joliot (1900–1958) build a cyclotron in France. He was teaching physics lab courses at Columbia when the war came. Soon after, he was at the Manhattan Project's Oak Ridge facility working on the problem of how to keep the diffusion barriers from deteriorating during the uranium separation process.

In 1948 Hugh joined the staff at Los Alamos as group leader in charge of critical assembly research. His group was charged with conducting "accidental criticality" studies—determining the point at which a given amount of radioactive material in close proximity results in spontaneous chain reaction. Thereafter, everyone at Los Alamos relied on Hugh's group to identify and mitigate health hazards involving fissionable materials. This responsibility ran the gamut of checking procedures related to storing, processing, fabricating, transporting, and research involving fissionable materials. In 1973 Hugh received an award on behalf of the critical experiments group for their part in the lab achieving 1.5 million man-hours of work without a disabling injury.

Soon after the war, the lab set up a program for graduate students in physics to go to Los Alamos to do their doctoral theses. From 1946 to 1947, John Allred (1926–96) was the first grad student to work under the tutelage of my father. After he earned his doctorate, he was hired by the lab and stayed at Los Alamos until 1953. He then went to the University of Houston, where he became head of the physics department and, subsequently, vice president of that institution. In 1978 John returned to Los Alamos and worked for the lab as a consultant until he retired. After retiring, he established a publishing company, Exceptional Books, Ltd., which published mostly nonfiction titles.

John spent a lot of time at our house, and we had an uncle-nephew relationship. In 1950, when I heard he was planning to get married, I was very upset because I thought that meant we'd be seeing a lot less of him. My distress was lessened significantly, however, when I met his wife-to-be, Elizabeth. She was gorgeous and sweet, and I have adored her ever since.

I suspect that many of the children who grew up in Los Alamos encountered lifelong pressure to succeed. John Allred was among those who felt strongly that once I graduated from law school I should practice law. However, I was adamantly opposed to doing so. He called me in December 1974, just as I was organizing the Office of Citizen Response in Denver. He said, "Terry, my aunt just passed away, and I'll pay you a million dollars if you will go to Texas for six months and oversee the attorneys handling the estate. I need someone there I can trust, and I sure as heck don't trust those attorneys." My initial response was, "John, I'm truly flattered and honored, but I don't know anything about estate law in Texas, and I am not licensed to practice law in Colorado, much less in Texas." John answered, "Terry, you don't need to be a practicing attorney. I just want you to go down there and keep an eye on them." I said, "John, I'm really sorry, but I just can't do it. I've just been given the responsibility of setting up and running a new city agency that could have a positive impact on the quality of life of the citizens of Denver. I wouldn't be able to live with myself if I backed out now." John reticently accepted that argument.

In 1994 John gave me my first computer. He had purchased a new system and didn't know what to do with his old one. He offered it to my parents, but they declined, so he wanted to know if I would take it. I was computer illiterate by choice, but I fought my apprehensions and agreed to take it. It proved to be extremely useful for the next five years, at which point I replaced it with a new system (given to me by another friend).

Every couple of years, John called me to get my opinion on some legal problem. I always prefaced my response with: "As you know, I can't give legal advice, but I'll be glad to discuss the problem with you as a friend, with the understanding that any so-called advice is worth every penny you're paying for it."

In 1996 John called me to discuss another such problem. In the midst of my usual pat response, he said "Terry, why wouldn't you ever practice law? They need an honest lawyer. They're all such SOBs." I responded, "John, that's just the point. To be an effective attorney in most venues, you have to be willing to be a 'real SOB,' and I never wanted to be an SOB." He never again raised the issue, but he passed away about six months later, so maybe he just never had the chance.

George Cowan first went to Los Alamos for a year in late 1945. He returned in 1949 and has been there ever since. He was a member of Fermi's group in Chicago that produced the first controlled chain reaction. He said there was substantial shielding on three sides of the reactor under Stagg Field, but the fourth side was up against a brick wall. They soon determined that the people who lived across the street from the brick wall could be receiving some radiation, so they moved the reactor to Argonne, where it later became the focal point of the Argonne National Laboratory.

George said that during the early days of the Soviet program to build an atomic bomb, they had not been particularly careful to protect their people from the effects of radiation (although the war was over), and they ended up losing a number of their scientists. However, he conceded that the same was true at Los Alamos during the Manhattan Project. The primary consideration was to get the job done as quickly as possible; safety was a distant secondary concern.

In 1946 George was in a B-17 flying over an atom bomb test in the South Pacific. They were guiding a drone B-17 through the mushroom cloud to collect data for analysis of the blast. There was a photographer in the bomb bay taking photos, and when the shock wave from the explosion hit them, it knocked the photographer out of the plane. Fortunately, he was tethered to the plane, and with considerable effort, they were able to drag him back in. I suspect that bungee jumping would be tame in comparison.

George is credited with helping to determine, from the examination of air samples, that the Soviets had detonated their first atom bomb in 1949. It came as quite a shock to most experts in the United States government, because they thought the Soviets were still years away from developing the bomb. Los Alamos promptly went back to a six-day work week, and the rush was on to build the hydrogen bomb.

In 1973 or 1974, George investigated the mystery of the depleted uranium ore that the French were getting from their mine in Gabon. The French thought it might be due to a natural cause, but for a time they suspected a conspiracy, thinking the United States might somehow be adding depleted uranium to their ore. George helped prove that the ore from Gabon was, indeed, depleted by the natural cause first theorized by the French. It seems the ore originally was so rich in U^{235} that about 1.8 billion years ago, groundwater seeped into the ore, causing a natural chain reaction. It probably continued on and off for thousands of years until the U^{235} became depleted and the reaction could no longer sustain itself. George further showed that, had the United States been filtering depleted uranium from U.S. reactors into the French supply line, there would have been measurable levels of U^{236} in the ore, but there was none present in the ore in question. The mystery was solved. George received the Enrico Fermi Award in 1990.

Mathematician Bill Beyer went to Los Alamos in 1959. Bill told me that he first saw my father in 1944 while he was meeting with his physics professor, Merit Scott. He said my father walked into Professor Scott's office dressed like a New York lawyer and began putting formulas on the blackboard and explaining to Professor Scott what he had done in his doctoral exam. After my father left, Professor Scott explained to Bill that "Louie Rosen just got his Ph.D." Bill then asked Professor Scott, "What is he going to do with a Ph.D. in physics?" Professor Scott replied, "Well, I understand he's going out west somewhere to work for the government." Bill's response was, "Gee whiz! You mean you can earn a living in physics working for the government?" Strangely, in all the years they were both at Los Alamos, Bill never told my father about this encounter.

When Bill first went to Los Alamos, he figured he would stay for a year or so. However, he was pleasantly surprised to find the lab being run by "talented and brilliant" people, and he ended up spending his entire career there. Bill was recruited by Stan Ulam to work in T-Division on the "Rover" project. Rover was intended to put a rocket ship into space using a nuclear-powered engine called "Kiwi." Bill said Stan was extremely imaginative and was the co-inventor of the H-bomb with Edward Teller despite his strong feelings to the effect that all countries should get rid of their nuclear weapons. Bill said that "Orion" also was Stan's idea. Orion was a project designed to facilitate the exploration of space by detonating atomic bombs in outer space to accelerate rocket ships. Both of these projects subsequently were scrapped because of concerns about the possibility of a mishap before the rockets reached outer space.

Bill spent years programming MANIAC II to solve mathematical problems; in fact, he ran the last program on it before it was shipped to the junkyard. He said MANIAC II was fast becoming unreliable because of hardware problems. He did a study and determined that if a program ran on it for fifty hours, there was a fifty-fifty chance that, somewhere along the way, the computer would make a mistake. The lab was going to give MANIAC II to the University of New Mexico, but the lawyers got into it and decided that government property could not be given to a university, so they had to just junk it. Bill said someone ended up buying it from "salvage" for $3,000.

As far back as I can remember, there has always been a "salvage yard" at Los Alamos. Anytime the lab was done using something, it went to salvage, where anyone could buy it for pennies on the dollar, and the salvage yard was infinitely more interesting than a hardware store.

Bill was the first person to clearly explain to me how Teller's original idea for a thermonuclear device, the "Super," was discounted based on mathematical analysis. It was only with suggestions from Stan Ulam that a functional H-bomb evolved.

Bill said Stan also had the idea of "mathematizing" proteins and the genetic code to reconstruct evolution. Bill devoted considerable time to that project, using Stan's technique of making a "metric space" out of all protein sequences, thereby making a hypothetical ancestral tree of all living things (of which the proteins were available to analyze). They later used the same technique on DNA after they learned what the DNA sequences were. This work was the precursor to the human genome project, and Bill found it astounding that, when all is said and done, the history of life on earth can be explained by mathematical formulae.

George Bell (1926–2000) was working on his doctorate under Hans Bethe, and Hans put him to work on some of the problems that Los Alamos was investigating even before George went to Los Alamos in 1951. Once he got his doctorate, he went to Los Alamos to work on the H-bomb, with the intent of staying for only a few years.

George told me about having lunch with Edward Teller and Hans Bethe shortly after he arrived in Los Alamos. Teller was, as usual, arguing adamantly that the H-bomb should be developed. His argument was that scientists shouldn't express political views or try to influence political decisions, but rather should do everything they could to achieve what the government wants them to. George was taken with the fact that this would be perceived by some as hypocritical given that Teller, more than most, had been successfully influencing political decisions for years.

George said that T-Division was rather amorphous, and he was one of a number of "floaters." The primary responsibility of floaters was to critique the work other people were doing and to pitch in on anything on which they thought they could make a contribution. George was one of the first to work on identifying the human genome.

George and one other person from T-Division were sent to Eniwetok, in the South Pacific, for a month or so to observe "Mike," the first H-bomb test, in 1952. They were to "serve as interpreters of theoretically based instructions." He said he doesn't recall doing much work, but they did a lot of snorkeling.

George was an accomplished mountain climber. He met his wife, Ginny, in 1954 when she attended a course he was teaching in Los Alamos on mountain climbing. He had just returned from an attempt to ascend K-2, the second highest mountain in the world. K-2 had not yet been climbed successfully, so his expedition would have been the first had they been successful. His party got to the 25,000-foot level and had to stay there for ten days without oxygen because of a storm. One of the people in their expedition was swept away by an avalanche, and his body was recovered forty years later when the movement of the glacier delivered it to the base camp. The rest of them suffered some irreparable brain damage due to prolonged oxygen deprivation at 25,000 feet. He said that, of the hundred or so people who have successfully climbed K-2, only about 70 percent have lived to tell the story. Furthermore, no one who was unable to get down under his or her own power has ever gotten down from K-2 alive.

George's wife, Ginny, was hired to work with an air force lieutenant colonel on "tritium analysis" in 1950. More specifically, they were trying to determine how best to flush tritium out of the human body. She said the lieutenant colonel used himself as the test subject, drinking tritium for the experiments, and he was able to determine that drinking water was the best way to rid the body of tritium. Everyone working with tritium was tested periodically, and when someone was found to have been exposed to the element, they were instructed to drink a lot of water.

According to my father, medical personnel had difficulty getting those individuals to drink enough water, but when it was established that beer was a satisfactory substitute, compliance rose dramatically. He said that one day a three-star general walked into the control room of the cyclotron, where the refrigerator was kept full of beer. The general saw Sergeant Stan Hall of the Special Engineering Detachment sitting at the controls with a bottle of beer. The general asked, "Sergeant, is that absolutely necessary?" Stan replied, "Sir, it won't work without it." Without another word, the general departed.

During the war, Don Rose worked at Oak Ridge before going to work at the Applied Physics Laboratory in Silver Springs, Maryland, doing rocket design for the U.S. Navy. When he arrived in Los Alamos in 1956, he worked on the project to develop nuclear-powered rockets. Subsequently, Don worked as a nuclear safety expert. Unlike Hugh Paxton, whose primary focus was criticality issues, Don worked on the analysis of hypothetical accidents involving nuclear materials for the dual purpose of determining how to avoid such accidents, and how to deal with the aftermath if they do occur.

For many years his wife, Mary Elizabeth, was one of my mother's regular golfing partners. Then, in the early 1980s, the Roses, the Rosens, and Nick Metropolis began a tradition of going to the Rio Grande Café in Española every Friday night to partake of their superb New Mexican and Native American cuisine. The men took turns driving, but the time came when Nick's driving was adjudged by the group's "resident safety expert," Don, to be inadequate. They told Nick that they had decided to honor the senior member of the group by relieving him of the responsibility of driving. Nick responded as follows:

> Okay, but I want to tell you a story. Long ago at the University of Chicago, there were three very bright students. Their common complaint was the inadequacies of certain professors who had outlived their former brilliance. All three of the students became professors, and to celebrate they gathered for a repast at their favorite restaurant. As they conversed, they decided to make a pact—that as soon as one of them started to decline mentally, the others would tell him. The years passed and one of the group began to show his age in the classroom. The other two decided that he must be told. At their next gathering at the same restaurant, the two concerned professors steered the conversation to the pact they had made years earlier. The friend about whom they were concerned exclaimed: 'You know, I have been meaning to talk to both of you about that very matter.'

That was vintage Nick Metropolis. He passed away several months later.

Herman Hoerlin (1903–85) first met his wife, Kate, after they escaped Nazi Germany via different routes for different reasons.

Herman escaped because he didn't want his scientific capabilities to benefit Hitler's Germany. Kate left Germany because the Nazis came to her house one day, took her husband at the time, Willi Schmid, out into the street and shot him. Willi had been a well-known music critic and the Nazis subsequently admitted they had killed the wrong Schmid. Rudolf Hess, one of Hitler's chief henchmen, visited Kate, apologized for the mistake, and guaranteed her a lifelong pension from the German government. I have known this story since childhood, but it is confirmed by a footnote in *The Rise and Fall of the Third Reich*.[3] Herman worked in J-(testing) Division on high-speed photography of atom bomb tests.

Alice Armstrong (1897–1989) worked for my father for many years and often shared our dinner table. Whenever I put an elbow on the table, she would say, "All uncooked joints off the table." I liked the way she said it so much that I sometimes slipped an elbow on the table just to hear her say it. Among the myriad experiments on which Alice worked with my father was the one that analyzed the Van Allen Belts. As a memento, my dad gave me a small, irregularly shaped piece of the insulation from the nose-cone of that rocket. It was orange, porous, and firm but not hard. Unfortunately, I think someone thought it was trash and threw it away around 1975 while I was incapacitated with multiple sclerosis.

Ken Erikson first went to Los Alamos in 1947 to do his doctoral thesis in physics. After he got his degree, he worked there for about a year before moving to Albuquerque and doing nuclear weapons-related work at Sandia Laboratory. Then, in about 1959, he became the president of Kamaan Nuclear in Colorado Springs.

In the 1950s, while he was living in Albuquerque, Ken dabbled in various entrepreneurial endeavors. One evening when we were visiting the Eriksons in Albuquerque, Ken took me with him to an auction. He explained how people bid by making almost imperceptible gestures. I was intrigued but afraid to move the whole time for fear my movement would be interpreted as a bid. It's amazing how many places on your body can develop itches when you don't dare scratch. Ken successfully bid on a clothes hamper full of rubber boots. I think he paid eight dollars for it. When I asked him why he bought it, he explained that if even one pair fit he would come out even. Unfortunately, the hamper contained thirty-six left-footed boots and no right-footed boots. Oh, well. At least he got a clothes hamper. Ken also bought surplus travel trailers and small houses at auction in Los Alamos and elsewhere. He would put them on parcels of land in the mountains and then sell them.

Throughout its history, LANL has attracted many of the brightest and the best scientists in the world. Those efforts not only helped to end World War II but have been invaluable to national security and international stability ever since. The work of the Los Alamos scientists has also made innumerable contributions to improving the human condition—to furthering our understanding of ourselves, of the world around us, and of the universe.

By describing some aspects of the personalities and of the accomplishments of a number of the Los Alamos scientists, I have tried to provide a sense of the culture and environment fostered by these gifted people. In retrospect, it is amazing to me not only that they made such major impacts on the future of civilization, but that they did so, for the most part, with such great modesty. For example, the revered Niels Bohr, the foremost pioneer in quantum mechanics, whose wisdom was recognized as second to none, was often asked to make a prediction on some weighty matter. He would typically preface his response with: "It is very difficult to predict, especially the future." He would then carefully proceed to render his opinion with numerous caveats.

While I was discussing this issue with my father, he commented to me that:

> Unfortunately that modesty, coupled with the secrecy required by much of industrial and government-sponsored scientific research, has come back to haunt all of science. It has fostered a culture of avoiding what is now a necessity—to explain in language that the general population can understand what it is that scientists do, how they do it, and why the interrogation of nature is so important to the future of the population of planet earth. Without it, the burgeoning population and diminishing resources of earth will unavoidably lead to disharmony between nations, and between people and their environment.

The "Atomic City"? Prove It!

At the request of Johnny Williams, my father agreed to teach at the University of Minnesota during the fall semester of 1949. We lived in a hotel the whole time, and I had to sleep in a *crib*! The Critchfields were living in Minneapolis at the time, and that's when their son, Bob, and I became friends.

One evening we went to visit Tom Roberts' family. Tom's father was finishing up his doctoral dissertation at the University of Minnesota, and my father was recruiting him to come to Los Alamos. When it was time to go we said good night, but we couldn't get in our car because the doors were frozen shut. I was impressed by the way my father and Tom's father resolved the problem. They found a syringe, filled it with alcohol, and gave the keyhole a shot to melt the ice. The Roberts moved to Los Alamos shortly thereafter, so Tom and I were schoolmates from first grade through high school.

In the spring of 1951, my father had to go to Eniwetok for several months for a series of bomb tests. Due to the length of his absence, my mother and I went to stay with her family in Tuscaloosa, Alabama, for the spring semester. He made any number of other lengthy trips to the South Pacific, but we stayed in Los Alamos on those other occasions.

Going to a movie was a pretty big deal when I was a kid. For a long time there was only one movie theater in town. Then, in the early fifties, a second theater opened but, as I recall, it closed sometime after I left for college. With the more recent rebirth of the movie industry, and all of the multitheater complexes being built, guess how many theaters Los Alamos has now? The answer is none.

I don't think they had any "trailers" about coming attractions back then, but the main attraction was always preceded by newsreels about such things as union strikes, the war in Korea, and the newsmakers of the day. Then there were the cartoons. There was Mickey Mouse, Tom and Jerry, Mr. Magoo, and my favorite, the Roadrunner. Finally came the serials like Flash Gordon. For us kids, the excitement of going to the movies was as much about the cartoons and the serials as the movies themselves. In fact, I seldom cared what the movie was unless it was a western or, a few years later, a war movie. Initially, I think the price of a movie was twenty-five cents, and popcorn was a nickel or a dime. Sometimes there were even double features. That was really neat! It meant spending all Saturday afternoon at the theater!

I started taking piano lessons in the third grade and continued for four years, although I hated every minute of it because I felt that piano was for sissies. However, when I started playing the trumpet in the sixth grade, my piano lessons came in handy. Thereafter, when I wanted to learn a song on the trumpet but didn't have the music, I could figure it out on the piano first and it wasn't nearly as obnoxious to listen to.

It was also in the third grade that we built a small model of the Taos Pueblo out of miniature adobe bricks. I did particularly well on this project because I had helped make real adobe bricks while working on Edith Warner's house. The significance of this is that it brought home to me that what you're taught in school can have practical applications.

Most of my parents' close friends in Los Alamos were scientists and their wives, including a legion of truly great scientific minds. With my parents' frequent entertaining, I quickly learned to mix with the learned. I had innumerable opportunities to converse with and, more significantly, to listen to these people discussing politics, science, sociology, and a variety of other subjects. I also got to play charades with them on numerous occasions. Few things are more enjoyable than watching brilliant scientists crawling around on the floor with a finger in one ear trying to get their teammates to guess "When, in the course (sounds like horse) of human events ..."

One night when I was about eight, my parents were having one of their many large dinner parties and, as usual, the guest list was a who's who of scientists. A balding man and I were eating at a card table in my bedroom, and I got into a discussion with him over the costs and benefits of someone like my father having no hobbies or activities other than his work. I argued strenuously for the benefit of having some non-work-related hobbies (such as playing ball with your kid). He argued just as strenuously on behalf of the position that if you enjoy your work, and if it is important, it's all right to work, work, work. "Your work is your hobby and your hobby is your work," he said. I had seen this person a number of times before, but I really didn't know who he was. The discussion became somewhat heated, and he became extremely red-faced. I marched into the kitchen and asked my mother, "Who *is* that man eating in my room with me?"

She responded, "That's Norris Bradbury, your father's boss, dear. Why?"

I answered, "Oh, nothing." I went back to my bedroom and tried to be more pleasant to "Mr." Bradbury.

Terry Anna's dad was an electrician, and he spent a couple of weeks working on the wiring for the Trinity test. However, I have been told that he wasn't there for the test, because he had to leave just beforehand with a bad case of the flu. In 1945 the Annas lived in Santa Fe, but they moved to Los Alamos in 1948. Terry Anna and I spent many hundreds of days together over the years. To avoid confusion, our families adopted the practice of calling us TA and TR.

From the age of six, TA's dad would often take me along when he took his family fishing or camping, so I learned about the out-of-doors at an early age. "Pop" Anna taught us one thing that I have come to believe is very profound: "Always leave your campground cleaner than when you got there." Expanding upon this bit of wisdom, I have found it a philosophy for life worthy of pursuit. I think it's impressive that this pearl of wisdom came not from any of the great scientists, but from an electrician.

During the summers, TA and I spent day after day scouting the hundreds of Indian caves in the sides of the volcanic tuff mesas around Los Alamos and shooting our BB guns at all kinds of things. In retrospect, we had a remarkably carefree childhood.

Once a year my parents would go in with a number of other couples and have a barrel of live lobsters flown in for a dinner party. I remember having lobster races with David Carlson down the kitchen floor before the lobsters got dropped in the boiling water. I always wanted to keep one for a pet, but no one ever took my proposal seriously.

Like everyone else, we used to listen to the radio before we had a TV. I especially remember Don McNeil's Breakfast Club and Big John and Sparky. I think Big John and Sparky were the first entertainers of national renown to come to Los Alamos. It seems to me that it was even before Los Alamos became an "open city," but I have no idea how they could have done so. I went to see them, and boy was I surprised and disappointed to discover that Sparky was a ventriloquist's dummy! I felt like I was the dummy, but I also felt like I had been "taken."

I think I was in the third grade when my father went on a trip to Australia. Before he left, he asked me if there was anything I wanted him to bring to me from Australia. I told him I'd really like to have a boomerang and a live kangaroo. I thought maybe I could ride to school (two blocks away) in its pouch.

When he got home he gave me a boomerang and a pelt from a joey. I have to admit I was a little disturbed by the pelt. It was really soft and pretty, but I felt bad for the baby kangaroo that had been killed to get it. Then there was the boomerang. I could never get it to work, so I concluded it was defective, and you know what you call a boomerang that won't come back to you, don't you? A stick.

The following summer I began taking horseback riding lessons once a week at Edith Warner's old house near the north end of the Otowi Bridge. About eight kids took lessons, and our mothers took turns driving us the ten miles each way. I only got in a few lessons that year because we left on a six-week trip to Europe in June.

One day the teacher had one more student than she had horses. However, she was boarding some Shetland ponies, so she decided to have me ride one of the Shetlands. I was the tallest kid there, and I was incensed. That thing wasn't even as tall as I was. It brought back memories of having to sleep in that crib!

As I attempted to mount, the horse was extremely skittish, so I was instructed to lead it to the arena and mount it there. When I mounted the horse, we discovered it had never been broken. It started to buck wildly, and I was initially extremely frightened, hanging on for dear life and yelling, "Help! Help!" My mother, whose turn it was to chauffeur half of the kids, was frantic on the sidelines. After a few minutes, the horse settled down and just ran around the arena. It was a really exciting adrenaline high. I was no longer frightened, just excited. I was enjoying it! After all, I had just "broken" a wild horse! By the time an adult got on a horse to rescue me, I didn't want to get off. However, the guy pulled me off anyway, and I didn't get to ride anymore that day.

In June of 1952 we left on our six-week trip to Europe. En route, I was proudly wearing my t-shirt that said "Los Alamos, The Atomic City." Some kid in an airport asked me about it, and I explained that Los Alamos was the town in New Mexico where the atom bomb was developed. First he thought that New Mexico was a foreign country and asked if they spoke English there. Then he wanted to know if there were still any wild Indians. Worst of all, he didn't believe me about Los Alamos and the atom bomb. I was somewhat indignant, and I got him to go with me to a gift shop to find an atlas. I showed him where New Mexico was but discovered that Los Alamos was not shown on the map. I don't think that kid ever did believe me. I'm sure that most Los Alamosans had similar experiences during those years.

On the way we stopped in Washington, D.C., and went to the zoo. While my mom was sitting down to rest for a few minutes, I went over to a large metal cage with a couple of birds in it. One of the birds started talking to me. I ran to tell my mother to come see the talking bird. Her initial response was, "Don't be silly, birds can't talk." I went back and chatted with the bird some more. After a few minutes, I went and begged my mother to come see it. She finally walked over to the cage, but the bird said nothing. As she turned around to go back to the bench, the bird said, "Whatcha standin' around for?" Somewhat piqued by the rather offensive tone of voice, my mother turned around and said, "Who said that?" The bird said, "Whatcha standin' around for?" My mom was clearly offended by the bird's attitude, but at least she acknowledged that it could talk. It was a myna bird, and it sounded a lot more human than any parrot I have ever heard. This was the first of many mind-broadening experiences provided by that trip. At every turn there was a reminder of how sheltered a life I was leading in Los Alamos.

We went to England first because my father had to attend a physics conference in Birmingham. I understand that Lise Meitner and Otto Frisch were there, but I don't know if I met them or not. In London there were still a lot of bombed-out buildings from the German blitz. Seeing that war-related damage was an eye-opening experience for me, even at that age. Having never experienced war firsthand, I think I assumed that as soon as the fighting was over, the destruction vanished. Food was scarce in England, and what there was of it was awful! I remember getting some mashed potatoes that I couldn't cut with my knife. One day we went to a buffet for attendees of the physics conference in Birmingham. The food was the best we encountered, but we saw one lady who just nibbled at it. We asked why she didn't partake more liberally of the plentiful offerings. Her response was sobering. She said, "I usually have very little to eat. My stomach has shrunk, and I no longer need to eat much to avoid feeling hungry. If I eat a lot today, it will just cause me to feel hungrier in the days to come."

We happened to be there at the time of Queen Elizabeth's coronation, and I still have a clear recollection of Queen Elizabeth in her gold-plated coronation carriage propelled by real horsepower. I remember numerous castles and museums, lots of torture chambers, the Tower of London, and the Crown Jewels.

When we went to Madame Tussaud's wax museum, it was not clear where we were supposed to purchase tickets. There was a "bobby" (English policeman) standing near the entrance, and my mom asked him several times where to get tickets. He said nothing. She got very irate and berated him for not answering her. I then approached him, touched him, and determined that he was made of wax. I told my mother, but she didn't believe me until my father verified it. Once inside, we saw a wax image of the Queen Mother, who had recently died of a stomach ailment. I saw her and said loudly, "Look, there's the lady who died of a tummyache!" Everyone glared. My parents pretended they didn't know me. I wasn't of the nature to be ignored, however, and the charade didn't last long.

In Amsterdam I helped dock workers unload large round Gouda cheeses. Stacked on the ground, they looked like piles of red and yellow cannonballs. The workers gave me a whole cheese in payment for helping them. I remember going to see The Hague. Our cab driver/tour guide spoke pretty good English but always pronounced the letter "u" as "you." He pointed out many "pewblic" schools and "pewppy dogs," but he did pronounce "tulips" correctly, and there were a lot of tulips. In the restaurant The Five Flies, I had roast duck with orange sauce for the first time. It was so outstanding that it remains one of my favorite meals today. Each table had little flags on it representing the countries of origin of the patrons sitting there. One very heavyset man epitomized the "ugly American" as he impatiently pounded his fists on the table demanding his dinner. We were terribly embarrassed that we were from the same country as he was.

To me, the most impressive thing on the entire trip was a fantastic miniature city somewhere in Holland. I don't recall just how large it was, but it sure seemed expansive to me at the time. Concrete walkways for visitors meandered through the little city, and there were buses, trains, and lots of other things in constant motion. Everything looked amazingly realistic. When I think about it today, I still think, "Wow!"

There was Paris and the Eiffel Tower. We lunched at the restaurant halfway up. When the bill came, my dad called the waiter over and said, "I think there has been a mistake. We didn't want to buy the place, just have lunch here." The waiter and my mother were not amused. I particularly remember the public restrooms in Paris. They were located on street medians and consisted of one long exterior wall with curved ends and a long trough. They were filthy, smelly, and as I recall, used by both sexes simultaneously.

Then it was on to Switzerland—Zurich and Geneva, Swiss chalets and cuckoo clocks. We went to Zermatt on a cog train to see the Matterhorn. No cars are allowed in Zermatt. The Matterhorn refused to show itself through the clouds until the last day. As we were getting ready to leave, the clouds dramatically parted and revealed a frightening-looking but truly majestic mountain. There was Interlochen and the glacier at Jungfraujoch with its permanent ice palaces, dogsled rides, and people walking around in shorts. I bought a small backpack, a cuckoo clock, and a Swiss army knife.

Although the clock stopped working years ago, I just had it restored for my son's family for Christmas. The Swiss army knife is in with my fishing gear. Then it was home with my mind full of impressive memories.

So if you question whether it is worthwhile to take an eight-year-old to Europe, the answer is an emphatic *yes!* It was a great learning experience that will not soon be forgotten. Although not unique, my European travels were unusual for an eight-year-old, even in Los Alamos, so when school started that fall I did a lot of public speaking, going to various schools and giving lectures and slide shows about the trip.

We were relatively slow to get our first TV. A lot of my friends families had gotten them, and I was feeling more and more left out at school because I couldn't contribute to any discussions regarding TV programs that had aired the night before. Finally, in late 1953 we got a little portable Zenith. We never put an antenna on the roof, because my mother thought they were unsightly, so we had to live with the poor reception provided by "rabbit ears." We were forever fiddling with them, trying to reduce the snow on the screen. Nonetheless, I got to watch TV an hour a day. My favorites were Roy Rogers, Gene Autry, Hopalong Cassidy, and the Mickey Mouse Club.

My fourth-grade class consisted of students who allegedly had high IQs, but we had no idea we were being segregated. We all lived in the Western Area, so it seemed perfectly normal to us that we were in the same class. I don't know what came out of the experiment, and I have no recollection of what we were taught that year.

In the fifth grade I had my first male teacher. He was extremely genial and a very good educator. I learned much later that he was also a binge drinker. Ten or fifteen years after he taught my class, he was still teaching at Los Alamos, and one Friday evening he and his good drinking buddy, a Los Alamos school principal, went to Santa Fe to get drunk. On the way to the bar, they passed the army recruiting center and the principal said, "Why don't we go in and sign up?" My former teacher said, "Oh, sure," as they walked on by. On their way back past the recruiting center many drinks later, the principal said, "Come on, let's go in and sign up." The teacher said, "Okay," and in they went. About six weeks later, the teacher went to the principal's office and said, " I got my papers to report. Have you gotten yours yet?" The principal responded, "Oh, my God! You don't mean to tell me you gave them your real name?" The teacher soon left to serve his country for three or four years.

Until February 18, 1957, every vehicle that went to Los Alamos had to stop at the "front gate." The guards there would check the identification badges of the "authorized personnel," and those who had badges had to vouch for everyone else in the vehicle. The guards sometimes searched the vehicle, although as time went on, the searches declined in frequency and thoroughness. However, if no one in the vehicle had a badge, the guards carefully searched the vehicle and denied entry until some authorized person came to the front gate and vouched for the occupants.

During the severe winter of 1944, Harry Allen, who was in charge of procurement for the lab, wangled some "zoot suits" (cold-weather coats) from the army for the scientists, most of whom walked to work. One of the top-echelon scientists lived in the same quad as Harry Allen. When that scientist left Los Alamos after the war, Harry noticed that he packed the government zoot suit. After saying many friendly good-byes the scientist and his family drove away, and Harry called the gate to tell them that the scientist was leaving with some government property. The guards searched the family's luggage and removed the zoot suit before allowing them to leave. The scientist, who was known to have a bit of a temper, was not pleased!

In the same vein, one of my cousins, Johnny Clements, came to stay with us for the summer of 1954. He and his mother arrived at the front gate and the guard asked his mother for her name. She gave her maiden name, "Edith May Terry." Johnny piped up, "But Mom, that isn't your name." She was interrogated for many hours before the guards called my parents and asked them to go to the front gate to straighten things out.

Although Johnny was two years older than I, we played baseball on the same little league team. Our coach was Tom Putnam,[1] a physicist and family friend. Johnny was more mature than the other kids, and with his many home runs he was everyone's hero, including mine. In fact, it was because he played the trumpet that I got interested in doing so. That summer Johnny became the first person to go through the human radiation counter. I became the second and my mother, the third.[2]

My dad bought a new rotary lawnmower that summer. At my insistence he carefully explained how to turn it off without getting a shock. Then he told me to turn it off. My finger slipped; I got a shock and it knocked me on my tail. When I looked up at my dad I had a stunned look on my face and he had a wry smile on his. Only my pride was hurt, but I gained a healthy respect for the spark plug.

For the rest of the summer I mowed our lawn under my mother's strict quality control. The following spring I showed TA how to work the lawnmower and we set out to mow, clip, and water lawns for other people. We called our business T & T Lawn Services. We were very conscientious about doing a good job and were busy from dawn to dusk every day for months (except for horseback riding, piano lessons, baseball practice and games, and occasional movies). We each made more than $1000 the first summer, and we did it again the next two or three summers. It sure beat delivering newspapers!

Just before I turned eleven, TA's and my parents allowed us to go bird hunting and camping overnight by ourselves for the first time. A schoolmate, Mike Zerwekh, was supposed to go with us, but he cancelled out at the last minute. One of our dads dropped us off in an isolated area just east of Buckman Mesa, about four miles southeast of the Otowi Bridge. I had gotten a beautiful, blond pump-action Remington .22 rifle for Christmas and was anxious to try it out. We spent the day shooting at rabbits and birds with my new .22 and TA's .22/.410 over/under shotgun. It was Christmas break, but it was a beautiful day. That night, as we were feasting on breaded fried shrimp, pork chops, and other wild delicacies, it began to snow and get cold. As we shivered between courses we would say repeatedly to each other, "Boy, I'll bet Mike is glad he's not here right now." Then, as we were devouring the next batch of goodies we would say, "Boy, I'll bet Mike wishes he were here right now."

After eating, we got into the tent, climbed into our sleeping bags, and drifted off. Sometime after midnight, we awoke to the sounds of muffled voices outside. We were scared, but were trying to "out-brave" one another, and we armed ourselves for whatever was approaching our tent. TA had his .22/.410 in one hand and a knife in his other hand. I had my .22 in one hand and a hatchet in the other. We could see some lights, and because we thought we might be on Indian land, we thought it might be Indians out to protect their land from trespassers. We didn't know if they killed trespassers or not.

We didn't make a sound, but we were ready! When the zipper on the tent began to move, we began to squeeze the triggers. Fortunately, we recognized my dad's face before we fired. It had already snowed eight or ten inches and our fathers had decided to come get us while they still could. It's a good thing they did, because the snow was eighteen to twenty inches deep by morning, and we might have been stranded for days.

We had no idea how bad the snow was until our fathers came for us, so we hadn't been at all concerned about the weather, but had they been unable to reach us that night, it could have gotten a bit dicey. Until I began writing this book, both TA and I had preserved our perspective as ten-year-olds that this had been a life-threatening situation. However, upon giving it some serious thought I have concluded that, although we might have gotten very hungry, our lives were probably never at risk. If necessary, my father could have gotten the army to rescue us—another benefit of living in Los Alamos at the time. Upon arriving home that night I had my first alcoholic beverage—a hot-buttered rum. I have had a few hot-buttered rums since, but none of them ever tasted as good as that first one.

After I turned eleven I joined the National Rifle Association, and for several years I went to the indoor shooting range downtown two or three times a week. By age thirteen, I had earned all of the "junior" marksmanship medals, and I was an alternate on the New Mexico State Shooting Team for .22 rifles for a couple of years thereafter.

I think I was eleven when well-known author Pearl Buck came to Los Alamos to interview scientists for a book she was writing. She spent a day at our house interviewing my father and she joined us for dinner. Ms. Buck had an excellent reputation and had received the Nobel Prize for Literature in 1938, but I couldn't find anything about her to like. She struck me as extremely pompous, loud, obnoxious, opinionated, and steadfastly attached to her hypothesis—that scientists, artists, poets, and the like are similar in that they are too unlike "normal" people to live with the rest of society (or something like that). She wasn't interviewing people to determine whether her hypothesis was valid or invalid. She assumed it to be valid, and was simply looking for evidence to substantiate it while disregarding conflicting evidence. It seemed to me, even at that age, that her approach was intellectually dishonest. I was very impressed with my father's restraint and his ability to maintain decorum in the presence of this horrible creature.

My parents used to play some bridge, and at about age six I became intrigued with the game. I would sit on my father's lap trying to figure out what was going on. That came to an abrupt halt the night I said, "Wow! Look at all those pictures!" My interest in the game continued, though, and by the time I was eleven or twelve, my mother would let me sit in for her while she was preparing hors d'oeuvres. Some of my friends also learned to play bridge, and by the ninth grade we had a foursome that played regularly. In high school, the bridge games often turned into penny-ante poker games when friends showed up who didn't know how to play bridge.

Once when we were short of poker players, we invited Bob Critchfield's father to join us. He had been drinking quite a bit and I told the guys, "Go easy on Charlie; he's had quite a bit to drink." Well, he wiped us all out in short order. I didn't realize Charlie was a world-class mathematician in addition to being a physicist.

I played little league baseball from age ten to fifteen. The summer when I was fourteen, I had fourteen home runs (in about sixteen games), and I lost only one game as a pitcher—the last game of the year. It was a playoff game to determine the league championship because both teams finished the season with identical win-loss records. We lost 1-0, although I pitched a no-hitter and played a direct part in seventeen of the twenty-one outs. During those six years of baseball, I have a clear recollection of my father having attended one game, and he left before it was over. That was the year I hit fourteen home runs, and I really wanted him to see me hit one. Needless to say, I was crushed when he left early. I explained to the other players how he had to leave because he was involved in a very important project.

Although I loved sports and had some aptitude for them, I got zero parental encouragement to pursue them. I don't think my dad ever saw me play any organized sports other than that one game. In retrospect, I wish I had said something to him instead of trying to hide my feelings about it. I didn't say anything for several reasons. I didn't want to admit that the lack of support hurt my feelings; I understood that, as always, my father was doing very important work, and I suspected that his lack of support was due to his not wanting to encourage my spending time doing things that he considered a waste of time. I was over fifty before I learned that he played basketball in high school. He may have told me previously, but if he did I'm sure I thought he was joking, because he was only five feet, nine inches tall.

When I attended my high school reunion in July 2000, I was putting the finishing touches on this book, and I discussed this issue with one of my former classmates. She suggested that I talk to the sons of other Los Alamos scientists to see if their fathers ever attended their ball games. I thought that was a great idea and said I would do so. Upon giving it some thought, however, I could only think of one other person who played baseball whose father was a scientist, and I have no idea how to contact him. It also occurred to me that, in those days, there were very few kids whose parents did attend ball games.

From the third grade through high school, TA and I, and sometimes others, spent innumerable nights camping out around Los Alamos. After we got our driver's licenses at age fifteen, we broadened our horizons and backpacked and camped all over the mountains of northern New Mexico. Whenever possible we would sleep under the stars, and sleep was often preceded by a lengthy discussion of God and nature. TA and I concluded that God and nature must be one and the same. My perspective has not changed much since.

– 9 –
Kaboom!

Given the manner in which Los Alamos was thrown together, the population was remarkably stable. Consequently, many residents had an opportunity to forge numerous deep and lasting relationships. Many of my friends and I went from grades six through twelve together with only minor interruptions.

Some of my closest friends were Terry Anna ("TA"), Bob Bergland ("Bob B."), Bob Critchfield ("Critch"), Wayne McCloskey ("Mac"), and Steve Robison. All of us but Critch went to school in Los Alamos together from at least the ninth grade, and TA and I attended the same schools from first grade on.[1] Critch, the only one of us born at Los Alamos, only attended school in Los Alamos for one year in elementary school, so we went to different schools together, but he and I remained friends nonetheless. He became close with the rest of the guys in what came to be called the "Good Friends are Forever" (G.F.A.F.) group later, mostly as a result of poker games and summer backpacking trips into the Pecos Wilderness in the years following graduation from high school. Roy Martin and Mike Bowersox ("Sox") would have been included in the G.F.A.F., but Roy didn't maintain contact with any of us after high school, and Sox pulled a vanishing act after joining the navy following his first year of college. I have heard a little bit about Sox, but we didn't make contact again until I got an e-mail from him in 2000.

The rest of us have stayed in touch over time, although Mac and Bob B. have been living back East for many years. In the summer of 1995, all of us but Critch attended the Los Alamos high school reunion—the first school reunion I had ever attended. After the reunion we all went fishing for a few days. Critch hadn't gone to the reunion because he didn't go to high school in Los Alamos, but he volunteered to precede us to the mountains and set up camp. One night while we were camping, I set up my camera and wrote "Good Friends Are Forever" in STAR WRITING™.[2] The get-together was so incredible that the name stuck, and we agreed to meet every other year "forever." To date, the level of commitment the six of us have shown has been nothing short of astounding! I find it curious that of all my close friends, the only one who ended up working for the lab for any length of time was Critch. In fact, as of 2000, Critch still worked for the lab.

My friends and I played a lot of "sandlot" sports throughout our schooldays. One day in high school when we were playing tackle football (without pads), Sox got tackled and broke his clavicle. It was forever after terribly misshapen, but that didn't stop him or us from playing football. I also played some golf growing up, primarily because my mother liked to play and she thought I should learn the game. My father played with us once in a great while— maybe six times in all. On one of those rare occasions, he hit a ball on a 200-yard par three, and it bounced and rolled on the dirt all the way from the tee box to the green and went into the hole. After that, it was even more difficult to get him to play. Whenever we suggested it, he would just say, "No, that game is too easy." My friends and I played some golf as we got older, but not on a regular basis. Mac's younger brother, Dennis, outclassed all of us and eventually turned pro. He has been the Los Alamos golf pro for many years now.

From the beginning, the serene mountain atmosphere of Los Alamos was often interrupted by resounding and sometimes earth-shaking blasts of explosives, testing for one thing or another. The frequency diminished over the years, but there is still an occasional blast of HE today. In fact, in 1977 Critch began working with the group that was responsible for many of those explosions, and after a few years in other divisions of the lab (including five in my father's MP-Division), he returned to that group.

As kids we became somewhat accustomed to the blasts and miniature earthquakes that sometimes accompanied them, but they always made us a little nervous. We never knew for sure if the detonation was just experimental or if some of our fathers had gotten blown up. This was not an unrealistic concern. As I mentioned previously, my father and many others often found themselves cradling fifty-pound assemblages of HE in their laps as their military drivers sped their jeeps over very rough dirt roads—certainly not the kind of risk that would be found acceptable in the workplace today. In my father's case, the driver was one or the other of the two army technicians assigned to his group—Myron Daley and Mike Clancy. You may recall that Mike is the person who got arrested when he borrowed my parents' radio so he could listen to the World Series.

I got a chemistry set for Christmas when I was eleven and soon learned how to make gun powder-based "rocket fuel" for little tinfoil rockets. TA and I made hundreds of them and always got a "blast" out of shooting them off. One day, after we had developed two-stage rockets, we decided to take a quantum leap and try to launch the casing of a .30-30 bullet. We packed it with fuel, attached a couple of tinfoil wings to it, and inserted a ten-second fuse. We put it on our launch pad—the concave side of a six-foot length of wooden molding leaning against the fence—lit the fuse, and ran around the corner into the garage. We waited and waited, but nothing happened. After a minute or so, we started to slowly approach our dud, when KABOOM! It was the most intense explosion I have ever heard. It startled the entire neighborhood despite everyone being accustomed to explosions, and it scared TA and me half to death. Neither of us could stop shaking for hours. The "rocket" went absolutely nowhere. It was lying on the ground right next to the "launching pad" with a half-inch-diameter hole in its side. Anyway, our quantum leap was not forward. That marked the end of our rocket-building days.

When Los Alamos became an "open city," my father saw a notice in the paper that the tanks—those stalwart metallic confederates of the gate sentries for all those years—were going to be auctioned off. He suggested that we go and bid on one, and I was deliriously excited about the idea. I mean, how many families with kids own a real "live" tank? My mother, however, was not favorably inclined—despite our suggestion that she could use it for a giant flowerpot. In addition, a prerequisite to purchasing one was that it had to be removed from Los Alamos within twenty-four hours, and we had no place to put it. Who am I kidding? The main reason we didn't try to buy one was my mother's opposition. Those tanks sold for $500 each.

Many of the early prefab houses were also sold at auction. After one auction, some buyers moved their purchases off "the hill" and parked them on Indian land. The next day, the Indians fenced in the area. The Indians had always been cooperative with the federal government but harbored some resentment against the "rich" folks at Los Alamos, and they weren't about to let such an opportunity slip by. The houses were no longer government property, and they remained fenced in for years. Some of those prefab houses had been purchased by Ken Erikson.

During the mild spring and summer evenings, I used to play hide-and-seek, kick the can, "Mother may I," croquet, and other games with the other kids in the immediate neighborhood—in particular Kay and Bobby Russell, and Steve Sydoriak. We also played a lot of checkers and Monopoly. I don't believe I ever lost a game of either one. However, I was the oldest of the group by a couple of years, and the negotiating skills of a ten- or eleven-year-old are far more advanced than those of children two or three years younger, so my winning was no major achievement. I didn't win every argument, however. When I was about ten I had an argument with Bobby Russell because he insisted that six plus six equaled eleven. No matter how I explained it, I couldn't get him to concede that he was wrong. I believe he now teaches math at the college level—quite competently, I'm sure.

When I was twelve, we (the neighborhood kids) organized a "Kid Carnival" to help raise money for the Community Chest "Red Feather" fund drive. We ran it for two weekends and raised over $25—not bad considering that we charged one cent per game. The newspaper article recognizing this feat is reprinted below. I'm the tall kid on the left.

THE NEW MEXICAN
Wednesday, October 24, 1956
Kid Carnival Helps Boost Chest Drive

LOS ALAMOS-The cooperation [of] Los Alamos with the Community Chest drive reached down to [a] youthful level last weekend when nearly a dozen neighborhood youngsters put together a back-yard carnival to assist in the Red Feather drive for funds.

The setting of the carnival is the back yard of the Steve Sydoriak house on 41st Street in the western area and the success of the past weekend has encouraged the youngsters to repeat it this weekend.

A large variety of games of skill are laid out and may be played for a very reasonable cost . . .[3]

KIDS TAKE NOTICE—IF YOU ARE LOOKING FOR A WAY TO RAISE FUNDS FOR THE Red Feather drive take a look at what some enterprising youngsters rigged up to help with the Los Alamos Community Chest drive. A group of children in the western area pose in the horror house which was a part of a back-yard carnival given to raise funds for the Chest. (Dan Elliott photo)[4]

It was about that time that my father went on a business trip to Germany. When he got back he presented me with a big, beautiful Grundig tape recorder—one of those that had two large reels and was a bit temperamental, kind of like a fine sports car. My father spent a lot of time recovering tapes from the bowels of that tape recorder. TA and I spent many hours talking and singing into it. I still have some of those old tapes but, even if the tapes haven't turned brittle by now, I suspect that it would be extremely difficult to find one of those old two-reel tape recorders on which to play them.

In seventh-grade science we learned about our solar system, frogs, and snakes. One day a rattlesnake bit our teacher, Mr. Lyons. He had an allergic reaction, almost died, and was out for nearly a month. I concluded that studying the solar system was a lot safer than studying snakes, because no one has ever been bitten by a planet.

Even in Los Alamos, there were school bullies and a little petty theft. In eighth grade I had shop just before lunch. I usually took my lunch to school, and three days in a row someone stole it from shop class. The next day I took a bag with two cat food sandwiches, each surrounded by a few grapes to make it look really enticing. However, no one ever took it, and after a week or so it started to smell up the shop. The teacher tracked down the source of the odor and demanded to know whose bag it was. I never owned up to it because I didn't want to give away the fact that I was trying to foil a thief.

During the eighth grade I saw Elvis Presley perform in a school gym (before he made it big time). The floor was open for dancing, but only a few people were doing so because most of the girls just crowded around the stage screaming and swooning. Although I later came to appreciate Elvis's talents, I really didn't like him that night. I resented the fact that all of the girls went crazy over him, and I thought his hip gyrations, with their sexual innuendo, were crude and low-class. You may remember that Elvis's nickname was "Elvis the Pelvis." My recollection was that this occurred at Los Alamos, but my friends insist that the biggest name to come to Los Alamos around that time was Chubby Checker. I have since determined that I must have seen Elvis on April 12, 1956, at the Armory in Albuquerque.

Although Los Alamos could never be confused with a major entertainment center, many of the early residents were very talented artists and performers. The local Little Theater group was outstanding! In addition, we did receive visits from a few entertainers of national renown, such as Max Morath (a foremost expert on ragtime), Yo-Yo Ma (cellist), and Rafael Méndez (trumpet player/composer).

In the ninth and tenth grades I played in the high school band. We traveled around the state to play at football games and for various band competitions. The band director, Mr. Helton, was an excellent teacher. We took first place in the state competition for marching and for concert bands both years (and for many years before and after that).

We also had the great fortune to have Rafael Méndez—one of the greatest trumpeters who ever lived—as an annual visitor to Los Alamos for many years. Rafael played Korsakov's "Flight of the Bumble Bee" so that it sounded like a trumpet trio. He had far and away the greatest range of notes of any trumpeter ever, and I suspect his record will never be challenged. Once when he was in New York City, he saw a newspaper article in which someone claimed the record for the greatest number of notes in one breath—400 plus. Rafael invited the reporter who wrote the story to his hotel. He beat the "record holder" by over a hundred notes. I doubt that record will ever be broken, either.

When he was ten, Rafael played for Pancho Villa, who took such a liking to him that he kept Rafael with his army for a number of months against his will. Rafael wrote a great deal of music, including over 300 trumpet solos, such as "Trumpeter's Lullaby." I describe his music as a distinctive and melodious combination of classical and jazz.

Rafael would stay in Los Alamos for several weeks, work with the band every school day, and cap off his visits by performing a concert with the band in the high school auditorium. During the concert he would play a trio with the two top trumpet players in the band. My sophomore year I got to play the trio with Rafael.

The Méndez concerts were a highlight of life in Los Alamos. Rafael did the same thing in many other communities throughout the nation, and it is still astonishing to me that he devoted so much of his time to helping aspiring musicians and enhancing the quality of life of others with disregard for the almighty dollar.

In 1957 or 1958, Queen Frederika of Greece and her daughter

visited Los Alamos. The high school band learned the Greek national anthem, and we got up early to give the queen a rousing musical greeting upon her arrival at 7:00 A.M. Unfortunately, it was well below freezing, and all of our instruments froze. Among the brass instruments, about one out of every six notes came out, and the sound was dreadful! My father gave the queen a tour of the lab, and he was quite impressed with her knowledge and understanding of physics. That evening, the queen and her daughter came to our house for dinner. I was embarrassed at having been part of the horrible racket made by the band, so I didn't mention that I had been there. Of course, my mother did.

The summer after the ninth grade, my parents sent me to a summer camp for a couple of weeks. I got Bob B. to take over my lawn-care duties for the duration and I went with Tom Putnam (Jr.) and his younger brother Greg (the sons of the physicist coach of my baseball team when I was ten). At the ranch, each boy had his own horse. The year before, on the last day of my horseback-riding lessons, my body had suddenly become allergic to a multitude of things, including horses. Due to my allergies, I couldn't go to the corral at the camp, but I couldn't pass up the allure of riding the open range, so I rode anyway. As long as the horse was moving, my allergy didn't act up.

Every day we rode to a swimming hole in the Pecos River or to a mesa with abandoned farmhouses. One day another kid and I pushed a big boulder off the top of the mesa just for fun. It rolled and rolled and rolled. There were some train tracks about half a mile away, and we became increasingly concerned as the boulder got closer and closer to the tracks. The tracks were up on a berm, and we reassured each other that even if the boulder went that far, the berm would stop it. It didn't. The boulder bounced over the berm, across the tracks, and rolled almost to the highway fifty yards beyond. At least it didn't stop on the tracks, but boy was that scary!

In the summer of 1957, the Santa Fe Opera came into being. Although I have never been much of an opera fan, I did attend the initial performance and went to maybe half a dozen other operas over the years. The quality of the performances was always superb! The opera was able to entice many famous opera stars to perform there because they enjoyed spending their summers in Santa Fe.

The Santa Fe Opera performs in an open-air theater, so its season lasts for only a few months each year. The back of the stage is open, so the backdrop is the beautiful Jemez Mountains. I attended one particularly impressive performance of *Jeanne d'Arc* during which there was abundant thunder and lightning in the background just when the script called for it—very powerful stuff!

During the summer of 1958, TA and I went on our first of many treks into the Pecos Wilderness. TA had just turned fifteen, and I was fourteen. Mike Zerwekh, who was almost an Eagle Scout, went with us. Our destination was Lake Katherine, the "Queen of the Lakes" in New Mexico. My mother dropped us off at the edge of the Pecos Wilderness and agreed to pick us up five days later.

Experienced as we were, we took such things as a full-sized ax, canned goods, fresh eggs, my heavy canvas "pup tent" (just large enough for three sleeping bags), and so forth. To carry our gear, we had one full-sized backpack, a little backpack I had gotten in Switzerland, and a large fishing creel.

Half a mile up the trail, we were crossing a stream when the full-sized pack split down the seam and everything fell in the water. We jumped in and saved what we could. We recovered almost everything except for spices, which, to save on weight, we had put in tinfoil. Now we had a real problem! How were we going to carry everything without the big backpack? As much as we disdained the idea of a packhorse, we concluded that was the only way we could proceed. We pooled our financial resources, and TA and I walked back down to get a horse while Mike stayed with our gear.

We found a stable and rented a packhorse. We told them we were headed for Lake Katherine and they showed us how to hobble the horse so he could feed but not run away. As we headed back up the trail, I walked ahead of the horse or way behind the horse, depending on the wind direction, because of my allergy.

When we got back to Mike, he was taking a nap. In our absence, he had packaged all of our food and gear into our three sleeping bags. Thinking we should let him sleep as long as possible, TA and I loaded the horse. All we had to do was sling the three sleeping bags over the horse's back and lash them down.

Then we awakened Mike and commenced our trek. When we got to Stewart Lake, we were so tired we decided to stay the night

there. We went to the far side of the lake through thick woods because there was a grassy meadow for the horse. We hobbled the
horse and unrolled our sleeping bags to unpack. Much to my cha-
grin, I found that Mike had packed all of the raw eggs in the bottom of my sleeping bag and every last one had broken. I got the
shells and most of the egg out, but it was dark and getting cold, so
I spent the night with freezing raw egg at my feet.

At 6:00 A.M. we awoke to the sound of a low-flying aircraft. We
quickly dressed, TA got out his camera, and we headed for the dam
at the far end of the lake. We saw a ranger standing on the dam and
we wanted to find out what was going on. Before we got there, the
plane made a low pass and dropped thousands of fingerlings into
the lake. Unfortunately, the pilot overshot his target a little bit and
the ranger got peppered with fingerlings. The plane made a second
pass, and this time the ranger got out of the way.

TA took some pictures, but the camera shutter had frozen
closed, so none of them came out. When we finally got to the
ranger, he asked us if we were missing a horse. We said, "No. Ours
is right over—hey! Where'd he go?" The ranger said we didn't have
to worry about it—that the horse knew the way home and was already halfway there.

Once again, we found ourselves with no way to get our gear the
mile or so to Lake Katherine, so we simply stayed at Stewart Lake. We
built a raft so we could fish farther out in the lake, but the fishing was
terrible, primarily because of the multitude of small new inhabitants,
many of which became sushi for the longtime residents. We did catch
five fish the first day, but we left them in the water overnight, and in
the morning they were covered with leeches. None of us had ever
seen a leech "in person" before. We had seen them in the movie
African Queen, but we didn't even know they existed on our conti-
nent, and there was no way we were going to eat those fish.

When it was time to go home, we found ourselves with all of
our gear, thirty feet of inch-thick rope, two large leather saddle
packs, a feed bag, a packsaddle, and no horse. To reduce our load,
we buried some surplus canned food, figuring we could pick it up
the next time we came.

We cut down an aspen tree in spite of our concern that we
might be breaking some law. We cut off the branches and tied everything to the pole except for what little would go in the creel and the

small backpack. Then we discovered that we couldn't get the pole through the thick woods because it was so much longer than the horse had been. Consequently, we had to put the whole load on our raft and paddle it across the lake. We got everything on the raft after nearly tipping over, but the load was so heavy that the raft was floating an inch under the water line. Then, when two of us got on, it sank another inch or so. Seeing no alternative, however, TA and I set out on the raft while Mike walked around the lake with the creel and the small backpack.

In the high mountains, the weather can change instantaneously. We were halfway across the lake when a thunderstorm hit, and lightning was striking everywhere. Realizing how vulnerable we were, we both lay flat on the raft (in the two inches of water) and paddled like crazy. We finally made it across, but how it was that lightning didn't strike us or the raft is beyond me.

Once we reached land and off-loaded the pole, two of us would lift and carry the pole (which weighed well over two hundred pounds), while the third carried the creel and small backpack. Then we would trade off and someone else would get to carry the creel and backpack. It rained during the entire trip down. At the beginning we would say, "One, two, three, UP!" to get the pole on our shoulders and would carry it fifty or sixty yards. After an hour or so of slipping and sliding in mud, we were saying, "One, two, three, four, five, six, seven, eight, nine, ten, UP!" and staggering with it for twenty or twenty-five yards. We were about halfway down when Mike and I came up with the idea of making a travois, just like the Indians used to do. The path was less rocky the rest of the way down and we were pretty sure it would work. TA didn't like the idea, but he finally agreed to sit down and rest while Mike and I made the travois.

We set about cutting down yet another aspen tree. Once we had cut it into pieces and lashed them together, Mike and I insisted that since we had done all the work, TA had to pull it first. We rolled up two sleeping bags lengthwise, tied the two ends of each one together (horseshoe fashion), and placed them crisscross over TA's head. Finally, we slipped the two poles of the travois into the loops of the sleeping bags.

TA didn't budge! He just turned green and dropped to his knees while saying in a highly strained voice, "Get this thing off of me!" Mike and I immediately realized the problem. We had placed the load at the top of the travois instead of at the bottom (so the ground would bear most of the weight). We explained to TA that it would just take a few minutes to fix, but he would have none of it. So we disassembled the travois, put the load back on the pole, and proceeded as before. By the time we got down, we had bruises halfway down our backs on both sides, and we couldn't stand up straight for hours.

When we finally made it back down, we went to the stable to check on the horse. He was fine, and we learned that the instructions we had been given for hobbling the horse were valid for Lake Katherine but not for Stewart Lake. It seems that the last quarter-mile to Lake Katherine is so steep that a horse will not attempt to get down while hobbled. However, at Stewart Lake, it's necessary to tie it to a tree.

When my mother picked us up, though we were covered in mud, she took us to Fiorina's in Santa Fe for the best pizza in the world! Thereafter, going to Fiorina's after trips to the Pecos Wilderness became a ritual. Mrs. Fiorina lavished us with samples of her daily specials before serving our pizzas, and she would ask us all about our trip.

Although we encountered numerous difficulties attributable to our inexperience, with time we became reasonably competent "backwoodsmen." In Los Alamos we lived surrounded by wilderness, and the out-of-doors was a big part of our life. The wilderness began only a block or two to the north, south, and west of our houses. Our extensive involvement with the wilderness instilled in many of us a love of, and respect for, the wonders of nature—feelings that have endured throughout our lives.

Whenever my parents gave an outdoor dinner party, I was charged with tending the barbecue grill, rotating the spit (no electric motors back then), and using a squirt gun on the fire when the flames got too high. I always enjoyed the parties, and as the meat-tender, I got to sneak frequent tastes of those wonderful roasts.

One summer evening when TA and I were fifteen, my parents had us serve as bartenders for one of their larger parties—fifty or sixty people. Many luminaries of science were there, including Edward Teller. Neither of us knew the first thing about mixing drinks, and when someone came up and asked us for a particular drink, we had to ask how to make it. That worked fine the first time around. After that, however, everyone mistakenly assumed we remembered how to mix whatever it was they were drinking, so we had to "play it by ear." Amazingly, no one complained about the drinks we gave them. However, a lot of people went home drunk, and a number of them stopped to tell TA and me that it was "the mosse interesting pardy I haf effer been to."

One day shortly after Bob B. got his driver's license, I went with him to drive his mom to Española. About four of the twenty miles to Española were known as "the roller coaster." The dips (arroyos)[4] were almost continuous and were severe enough to make your stomach rise when you dropped into them. Bob's mom rode in the back seat, and when we got to the "roller coaster," Bob's mom kept telling Bob, "Go faster! Go faster!" He did so, and when we dropped into the biggest dip, she clonked her head on the roof. Cars didn't have seat belts then, and she was knocked out cold. At first we thought she was dead. It was pretty scary! Fortunately she was still breathing, and after about a minute she came to. We drove into Española, bought some aspirin for her headache, and went back home. Bob's mom didn't ask him to go faster over the dips on the way back.

During lunch at school we, like the lab scientists, had a somewhat amorphous group. There was room for ten or twelve students at a table, and about half of the "good friends" group were there almost every day—especially TA, Mac, and myself. Sometimes, if another member of the chess club was in the lunch line next to me, we would play mental chess while we waited in line, but the chess club guys didn't particularly want to sit with the rest of my friends for lunch. Every day, TA's mother put a hardboiled egg in his lunch, and whenever Kent Waterman joined us for lunch, TA cracked his egg on the top of Kent's head.[5] Kent was a football player, and he was an extremely nice guy who was pretty laid back. He didn't appreciate TA's ritual, but he abided it. Well, one year, on the first day of April, TA's mom put a raw egg in TA's lunch. You know what happened next. What a mess! Kent wasn't so laid back that day!

Despite the extraordinary ethnic diversity of the population of Los Alamos, there were very few Blacks in town. I'm not aware of their having experienced any racial discrimination, but I do recall a

row at the barbershop at some point in the '50s when a barber refused to cut the hair of a Black man. Everyone was incensed at hearing about it and demanded that the barber be fired, but I think it
turned out that the barber just didn't know how to cut hair that
curly and didn't want to risk making a mess of it.

My father received a Guggenheim Fellowship to work at the French
atomic energy facility at Saclay, so after my sophomore year of high
school, my parents and I went to Paris, France, for a year. Initially
I was strongly averse to going. I was going to miss all my friends,
and I was batting .750 in "Police League" baseball—I had a single, a
double, and a home run in four at-bats. The trip also pre-empted
my making another attempt to get to Lake Katherine that summer.
TA and I tried to work it out so I could live with him for the year,
but my parents wisely insisted that it was too great an educational
opportunity for me not to take advantage of it. They were right.

I had never kissed a girl, and, thinking I needed to learn how to
kiss before going to Paris, I invited Rodell Sharp out on a date.
Rodell was a very nice, lovely blonde who was very popular and
dated a lot. At the end of the evening, we kissed goodnight. It
was such terrific kiss, I got dizzy and almost fell off the porch.
Nonetheless, I went home feeling very self-satisfied. Not only had
I learned how to kiss, I had learned about the potential power of a
good kiss. I will forever be in Rodell's debt for that lesson.

– 10 –
Belle Paris

Our trip began in a roundabout manner. We first went to Tuscaloosa, Alabama, for about a week to see my mother's family. We left our car there and took a train to New York City. There we rented a car and went to my father's parents' home near Loch Scheldrake, in the Catskill Mountains not far from Montecello. After a week there we returned to New York City and from there crossed the Atlantic on the luxury liner the *Liberté.*

I. I. Rabi and his wife were onboard, but they traveled first class and we didn't see them the whole time. Dick Garwin and his wife were also onboard. Dick is credited with having done much of the design work on the first hydrogen bomb. I don't remember them well, but we had dinner together several times during the trip.

Once we got to Paris we rented a Citroën "Deux Chevaux" (two horsepower). The Deux Chevaux was so small that you could park it almost anywhere. It was kind of like a tin can on wheels. On the convertible version, you just rolled the canvas top up on a metal bar, exactly like opening a can of sardines. Several times we saw people drive diagonally into a particularly tight parking space, walk around to the rear of the car, and bounce the rear end up and down to shift it over next to the curb. The car got great mileage, though. That was important because, even then, gas was the equivalent of about two dollars a gallon throughout Europe.

After a three-week hunt, we found a place to live. It was a second-floor apartment right across the street from the Bois de Boulogne (akin to a large city park). We liked the location because it was so convenient to everything. It was less than a mile from the school I attended, and there was a Métro (subway) stop just outside the front door. There were stores nearby for all of the necessities, and once a week a farmer's market set up a couple of blocks away.

The first time my mother went to the farmer's market for fruits and vegetables, she discovered that, unlike in grocery stores in the United States, you can't pick and choose your produce—you tell them what you want, and you have to take the bad with the good. She started picking up some of the tomatoes to look at them, and the owner shouted at her, "*Ne touchez pas! Ne touchez pas!* (Do not touch!)"

Once a week, farmers from all over would bring their produce into Paris and unload it on the streets at Les Halles ("the markets"). There were piles of vegetables ten feet high all up and down the streets. The truck drivers would usually eat and drink in the local bistros and party until 3:00 or 4:00 A.M. One place, in particular, was a lot of fun. The opera house was nearby, and after the opera was over the singers would often go to the restaurant Le Pied de Cochon ("the foot of the pig"). They would sing and dance all night, and the truck drivers would get up and dance on the tables with them. It was incredible!

Opera was an integral part of life for Parisians. It was not just for the wealthy. In order to assure that everyone who so desired could attend, a ticket in the upper balconies—standing-room only—could be had for the equivalent of about a dime. Nonetheless, not being an opera fan, I only went a few times. I do recall being impressed that they had a live horse onstage at one point during a performance of *Carmen*.

After finding a place to live, we set out to buy a car. We ended up buying a Triumph Herald sedan right off the World Showcase of Cars on the Champs Élysées. It was a wonderful little car! It did so well by us that, when it was time to come back to the United States, we shipped it to New York so we could drive it home.

I was a high school junior and attended the American School of Paris (A.S.P.). Like our apartment, the school bordered on the Bois de Boulogne. Only half of the students were Americans, and the student body of some two hundred (grades seven through twelve) included students from over thirty countries. Only about half of the teachers spoke English and, as I recall, the principal, the senior math teacher, and the American History teacher were the only Americans employed by the school. The whole school consisted of one very large three-story house.

In the mid-1950s, Los Alamos High School was named one of the top ten high schools in the United States. Consequently, I thought I would do well at A.S.P. We got report cards every six weeks, and at the end of the first six weeks I got all C's and one D. My parents and the principal were horrified, but they weren't nearly as surprised as I was. I had been studying reasonably hard and thought I was making satisfactory progress. I had always gotten A's and B's, and it was a real shock!

The principal called me into his office and told me that he expected much more from me. That discussion was very disquieting for me, and for the next several months I studied forty to fifty hours a week. By the end of the year, all but one of my grades were A's. I was especially pleased with my progress in French, because the teacher was determined not to give me a grade better than C. I improved that grade from a D to a B+. After that year, getting through my senior year at Los Alamos High was a breeze.

Given the nature of Los Alamos, it is not surprising that I had already taken every math class offered at A.S.P. except for "senior math." Consequently, I took the senior math class. Unfortunately, the teacher didn't have a strong math background. The course consisted of him presenting us with problems from math publications as our homework and discussing possible solutions in class. Most of these problems had never been solved by anyone, and we were graded not on the answer, but on our approach to the problem. On one occasion I couldn't figure out how to try to solve the problem, so I presented it to my father. He worked on it for about twenty hours and arrived at a solution. However, I didn't understand the solution well enough to explain it to the class, so I just gave his twenty-page proof to the teacher. Unfortunately, the teacher didn't understand it, either.

Over Christmas break, we drove our Triumph all over Italy. We visited Florence, Rome, Naples, Pompeii, Venice, and many points in between. On our way back north, we went to Milan. My father gave a lecture at the University of Milan, and a fairly attractive female professor showed us around the city.

Before we met with the professor I was cautioned to watch what I said, because she was a communist. I was astonished! At the time, my perception of a "communist" was synonymous with "dangerous criminal." I couldn't fathom that being a communist in Italy was not illegal. After all, ever since I could remember, the primary objective of Los Alamos had been to keep the communists at bay, with the constantly reinforced perception that our failure to do so would likely result in the annihilation of our way of life, if not of the entire human race. "Better dead than red!" we said. I wasn't even aware of the fact that there were any communists outside of the Eastern Bloc nations and (for the last year) Cuba except for visitors. I asked my parents why we were going to be consorting with a known communist in a country that was an ally of the United States. Their response was uninformative, however, so I simply did as they instructed and avoided politically controversial issues while we were with "the communist."

At one point we went to England for a week. We did some shopping and attended what I believe was the London opening of *My Fair Lady* with Rex Harrison. The queen was at the performance, and whenever the queen stood up we all stood up and remained standing until she sat down again. We also did the museum thing again, which got a little old, but at least this time the food was a bit more plentiful. I have always thought it was pretty amazing that I've been to England twice and I got to see the queen both times. Of course, that and $5 will get me a cup of coffee almost anywhere.

Over spring break, we drove to Normandy and down the coast to Mont St. Michel. It was the off-season, and the hotels were almost empty. In Normandy I wandered along the beach and investigated some of the concrete bunkers built by the Germans to defend against the anticipated Allied invasion. Although World War II had ended fifteen years earlier, there was still a strong stench of death in the bunkers. During the D-day invasion, Allied ships had towed a lot of hollow, rectangular concrete platforms across the English Channel to set up a system of roads out in the water so they could unload materiel. Each platform was about the size of a bus, and a number of them were still sticking out of the water, even at high tide. There were also numerous sections of land posted, *"Champs de Mines. Interdit"* (Minefield. Do not enter). I was astonished! Fifteen years after the war and there were still live mines lying around!

After visiting the memorable Mont St. Michel with its fascinating multitiered monastery, we took our time zigzagging through the "château country." We visited Orléans for a day, and traversed the wine country on the way back to Paris.

On weekends I sometimes went on strolls through the Bois de Boulogne. One day as I was doing so, I noticed that some guy was selling burro rides, and one of the burros had spooked and run off with a little kid on it. The kid was none too happy about it, and I could identify with that. The child's mother was in a panic and crying, and there were six or eight people chasing and screaming at the burro. I could see that the people had frightened the burro, so I quickly got in front of the burro, started talking to it very softly, approached it very slowly, and grabbed the reins. For those who saw it happen, I was their American cowboy hero. Did that qualify me as a "horse whisperer?" Hardly.

I was only fifteen but was enthralled by a nineteen-year-old senior, Iren (pronounced "eeren") Kiss Enevold. She was a gorgeous Hungarian refugee who, with her mother, had escaped from the 1956 Russian invasion of Hungary. I put Iren on a pedestal, and although she made a move on me one night, it didn't sink in until much later. Due to my mother's attitude about sex—she considered it an inappropriate topic for conversation—we never discussed it, and I was uneducated on the subject beyond having kissed Rodell.

One evening when Iren and I had a date, I bought some flowers to take to her mother, whom I really liked. I found some beautiful, large white flowers. They had large, hollow stems that were full of water, so I was a bit concerned about how they would fare being out of water for an hour or so. However, the flower lady told me that as long as I held them with the stems up they would be fine. She placed a bit of tinfoil around the bottom of the stems, wrapped them in paper, and pinned the paper with straight pins.

I had to take a forty-minute bus ride to the suburb of St. Cloud to get to Iren's house. It was rush hour, and the buses were absolutely jammed! You always got on a bus at the rear, paid your fare to a person in a little booth in the back, and moved forward to find a seat. The seating was like you see in pictures of European trains but without any walls between compartments. There were two people facing one way, and the next two facing the first two.

I paid the fare and got pushed down the isle by the crush of the crowd. When I got to the middle, I grabbed a pole and let the throng push me toward the center door. I positioned myself next to the accordion-style door, and after it closed I moved even closer to it. In order to protect my flowers I wanted to make sure no one got between me and the door. Everything was fine until the next stop. When the door opened, I had to lift the flowers shoulder high to keep them from being crushed. As soon as the door closed, I lowered them again.

After a few stops, the people behind me started giggling. I looked around and saw that the lady sitting with her back to me had a beehive hairdo with so much hairspray on it that it was waterproof. Right on top there was a puddle of water. I looked at my flowers, and sure enough, the tinfoil had fallen off. Every time I had lifted the flowers, water had run out of the stems onto this lady's hairdo.

Just as I realized what was happening, the door opened again. I raised the flowers again, trying to keep more water from falling on the hairdo, but one of the straight pins came off on the inside of the paper and slid down the paper and right down the back of the lady's dress. Now I had a real quandary! Should I tell her about it, or should I do nothing? The door closed, and I lowered the flowers again.

I was still pondering my dilemma when, just before the next stop, the bus driver had to break suddenly for some reason. The lady's head jerked a bit and she got splattered by the water on her hairdo. She was understandably startled and let out a little yelp as she stood halfway up and then sat back down. Unfortunately, when she sat back down, she sat right on the pin and jumped up with a blood-curdling scream! She had noticed the other passengers laughing, and now she had some idea of what they had been laughing about. She turned around, saw me with my flowers, and took a swing at me with her umbrella. I dodged the umbrella, but she started trying to get out of her compartment to come after me. Fortunately, the bus was so full that it took her ten or fifteen seconds just to get into the center aisle. By that time, the bus had arrived at the next stop, the door opened, and I jumped off. I thought about how lucky I had been that the bus was crowded.

I caught the next bus and got to Iren's house in St. Cloud (a Paris suburb) about twenty minutes late. I handed the flowers to her mother; she took one look at them, said "Hmmpf," and walked off. She didn't speak to me again for months and she was always cool toward me after that. It turned out that the flowers I had given her (lilies) constituted a serious insult, as the primary use of such flowers is for funerals. Apparently I was unintentionally insinuating that she was deathly boring or something. We didn't learn these things growing up in Los Alamos. So when you decide to "say it with flowers," be sure you know what message you're sending

One Friday night I went to a party at the home of a classmate whose last name was Simonet. My parents drove me to her house out in the country. It was a huge mansion with a four-car garage! The butler took my coat in the entryway, and I followed him down a long hallway to the living room, which was large enough to be a ballroom. There were about fifty schoolmates already sitting around the perimeter, and more showed up after I got there. She had invited everyone from the ninth grade up, and most of them came. Amongst the chairs were a lot of glass china cabinets full of sterling silver tea sets and sets of fine crystal. It reeked of old money. This was opulence such as I had never seen! There were no poor people in Los Alamos, but nobody I knew had money like this!

In Los Alamos, no one had servants (although many did employ maids once a week). The economic status of the residents of Los Alamos was perhaps most aptly described by a longtime resident who said, "If you hang out at the grocery store long enough, you'll eventually see everyone in town."

Before long we were told, "Dinner is served." We all moved into the dining room, and it was almost as big as the living room. It was set up as a buffet, with two, thirty-foot-long tables piled high with food. There were two of the largest hams I have ever seen, huge roast beefs (thirty or forty pounds each), and a couple of good-sized pigs, apples in mouths and the whole nine yards. To say it was lavish does not do it justice.

After a sumptuous meal, we were invited into a part of the house consisting of a series of smallish darkened rooms, with a few steps down from each one to the next. One of the rooms was the library, and I spent some time there perusing the books. A particularly handsome set of wine-colored books, volumes one through twelve or more, were all about Saint Simonet. Yes, my wealthy classmate was descended from a saint!

Another Friday night I had a date with Sue—a cute, petite senior whom I often joined at a sidewalk café after school with several other friends for a café au lait and a pastry. Sue was the daughter of a Soviet diplomat. I arrived at her family's large apartment, met her parents, and was escorted by her mother to Sue's bedroom. The door was closed, so I knocked and she said to come in. She was wearing a chiffon robe and a see-through nightgown. It was quite obvious that she was interested in making whoopee—not in going out to a movie as I had planned. She removed her robe and lay down on the bed in a very provocative manner.

I was still inexperienced in this area and was quite taken aback. I liked Sue, and I didn't want to offend her or have her think I was gay like one of her other friends was. On the other hand, I had no desire to go to bed with her. It also occurred to me that it might be a setup. Pictures might be taken and used to try to get my father to reveal nuclear secrets to the Soviets. That may sound pretty far-fetched, but bear in mind that this was during the height of the Cold War. My father had recently given a talk to the student body, so they all knew who he was, and they knew he had worked on the first atomic bomb. Anyway, after considerable stammering, I went out on the balcony and said, "It's a beautiful night." Sue got up off the bed, put on her robe, and joined me on the balcony. I figured that if there were a camera somewhere, it probably wouldn't see anything on the balcony, so I kissed her.

The approach I took worked. The rest of the evening we just played records and talked. I don't recall what all we talked about, but we didn't go out, nor did we do anything else of a sexual nature. After a few hours I thanked her for a lovely evening and left feeling very relieved. I was rather proud of how I had handled the situation, but for a variety of reasons I would not have felt right talking about it candidly with anyone. My father first learned about the experience when he read a draft of this book. After he read it, I asked him if my analysis of the situation at the time was sound, or if I had been overly paranoid. He said he thought that my perception was not unrealistic.

By March I had begun thinking and dreaming in French, and shortly before we left Paris I had my most satisfying experience of the year. A non-Parisian Frenchman stopped me and asked for directions. I obliged, and he asked if I was a native of Paris. When I told him, *"Non, je suis Americain,"* he was flabbergasted. It has now been over forty years since I left Paris, and I have forgotten most of my vocabulary but I still have a pretty good French accent—something most Americans never achieve.

On our circuitous route home from Paris, we took a train to Copenhagen and spent a few days there. Then we flew to Iceland and on to New York on a ramshackle DC-3. We arrived back in New York in early June and went to the docks to pick up our Triumph. We drove back through Alabama so we could pick up our other car, and we drove both cars back to Los Alamos.

Although I hadn't wanted to go to France, after we had been there for a couple of months, I loved it! I wouldn't have minded staying for another year. Paris has a very ethnically and culturally diverse population, and for the first time in my life, most of the male adults talked about things other than math and science.

I did perceive some prejudice in France—both toward the French by others, and by the French toward others. Many of these attitudes appeared to be rooted in pre–World War II events. I have always taken pride in the ethnic diversity of Los Alamos and the fact that there were few detectable signs of prejudice based on race or creed. Until I went to Paris, I had only a vague idea of the meaning of prejudice. During the year in Paris, I came to realize just how ignorant I was of the ways of the world.

That year in Paris was the single most significant element in my educational development. The interaction with peoples of diverse backgrounds; the museums; the different ways of the French, to which I had to adapt, have all proved invaluable. Just "being there," to borrow the title of a Peter Sellers movie, was exceptionally enriching.

What to Be? That Is the Question

Once we got home from Paris, I couldn't wait to see all of my friends. In addition to the G.F.A.F. group, there were a great many other guys and girls in our extended network of good friends. We often went on group outings, like tobogganing at night (although not so much during the summer). One of the girl's fathers owned a cabin in Aspen, Colorado, and during our senior year, six or eight of us made at least one weekend trip there for skiing. There was no hanky-panky—it was truly good, clean fun.

My senior year, a number of people tried to get me to run for class vice president. However, I detested the idea of becoming a "politician," so I declined. Instead, I agreed to be the stage manager for the Senior Varieties show. I don't recall much about it except that it involved a lot of hard work and was a great success.

The American School of Paris didn't have a band. Although I had practiced some in our apartment using a mute on my trumpet, my skills declined significantly over the year, so I decided not to play in the band my senior year. I was afraid I wouldn't be able to get back to the level necessary to play the trio with Rafael Méndez. I regretted that decision when I attended the Méndez concert and thought about what might have been. I did play in a small dance band that year, but I only joined them for three or four events. I did my first "professional" singing during those "gigs."

Alois "Louie" Cernicek was my favorite teacher throughout my years of education. He was my high school French teacher as well as faculty advisor to the high school chess club. He was a true linguist, who spoke eight languages including ancient Greek, plus a bunch of dialects. He had been in the Czechoslovakian underground fighting against the Nazis, and then against the communists. He was imprisoned by the Germans at least three times but always managed to escape.

Louie had earned a B.A. from the University of Masaryk in Brno, Moravia, and when he arrived in the United States in 1950, he gained entrance to the University of Chicago to pursue a master's degree in Soviet studies. He began his post-graduate studies by learning English in eight weeks. Shortly after he arrived in Chicago, foreign students were asked what their favorite language was, and since he had just arrived from Italy, he said, "Italian." Consequently, he was invited to the house of an Italian-speaking professor for Easter dinner. Several years later, after moving to Los Alamos, he learned that he had spent that Easter with Enrico Fermi and his family. Louie eventually earned a Ph.D. in linguistics from Georgetown University.

Louie first went to Los Alamos in 1954, and in addition to teaching high school French, German, and Russian, the lab relied heavily on his language skills to translate foreign scientific papers. He was a very good chess player and was the only person I knew other than Stan Ulam who could "give me a game" on a regular basis. Of course, this doesn't include the grand masters, but they were "one-shot deals." Louie was an excellent teacher, but we students quickly learned that we could delay quizzes for a day by sidetracking him into talking about his days in the Czechoslovakian underground. He sometimes spent half of the class regaling us with stories of his escapes from German prison camps.

While in Paris, I didn't play a single game of chess, so it took awhile to regain my skills after I got back. Almost every day after school, I would play as many games with Louie as he was willing to play. Initially, he routinely defeated me resoundingly. However, as the year wore on, I got to the point where I could beat him more than half the time. During the second semester, I played the best game of my life against him. In a very complex middle game, I was able to proclaim that I had a checkmate in six moves and showed him what those moves were. He carefully studied the situation, not believing I was right. He wasn't convinced until we were two moves away from the checkmate. Louie and I continued to maintain a close relationship throughout our lives.

Louie was largely responsible for the rise in popularity of soccer—especially girls' soccer—in New Mexico during the latter half of the twentieth century. He was still coaching soccer into his seventies. In 2000, the community recognized Louie as a "Living Treasure of Los Alamos."

In the spring of my senior year, I went out for the tennis team. There were only eight of us, and since eight players were needed for a team, my making the team was never in doubt. I was the newest team member, so I was initially ranked eighth. I had no idea how my skills would stack up against the other members of the team. As in band, you could challenge the person immediately ahead of you once each week, so I challenged the person ahead of me every week, and in six weeks I was ranked number two. Thereafter, the player initially ranked number one and I played a challenge match every week, and we usually changed positions about every week. That player was Mike Perotti, and he was superb at getting to and returning everything you hit, despite the fact that he had severe disfigurement of his elbows and knees due to a serious bone disease. Like Bobby Riggs, he was an aficionado of "the lob," and his determination was truly inspirational.

Other than Mike Perotti and myself, Sox and Steve were the best players on the team. Steve's game was enhanced by the fact that he was ambidextrous. In his fifties, Steve still played a strong game of tennis. In 1998 he was diagnosed with lung cancer; they operated immediately, and he was back on the tennis court in less than two months.

My senior year I made it to the state tournament in doubles, but my partner, Sox, and I were eliminated in our first match. I could blame it on the fact that Sox had a ferocious temper, and after he double-faulted several times during his first service game, his game (and ours) went down the tubes. However, we would have lost anyway, because our opponents were better than we were. They ended up winning the state championship. Like skiing, I pretty much gave up tennis after I graduated from high school.

In the early 1950s, Mike Perotti's father, Lou, who owned a

modest restaurant in Los Alamos, organized "Perotti's Clowns," a five-man softball team. Although I believe they all had full-time jobs, they were softball's version of the Globetrotters. The pitcher, "Bun" Ryan, was incredible! His pitches were clocked at over 100 mph. The first time someone tried to clock the speed of his pitches, radar guns had just been developed, and on the first pitch he hit and shattered the radar gun. Each game, he pitched to at least one batter from second base, and to at least one batter blindfolded! The fact that there were only five men on the team didn't matter much, since opponents seldom made contact with the ball. The Clowns' overall record was 177 and 23. My friends and I went to their games whenever we could. They were always fun to watch—especially when Bun pitched a cantaloupe instead of a softball.

According to Lou, when the Clowns were first organized, they all agreed that they would continue to play either for twenty-five years, until they had played 200 games, or until they had raised $200,000 for charity. It just so happened that they broke all three barriers at precisely the same time.

In April of my senior year, my parents went to Mexico for a week. While they were gone, some of us decided to have a party at "my" house. We made some punch and rounded up some beer and snacks. We didn't have any illegal drugs. I don't believe any of my friends ever tried any illegal drugs during high school (beyond a little underage drinking). If they did, I was certainly never aware of it, and I think the word would have gotten around. I wasn't even aware of the existence of illegal drugs other than marijuana until I went to college. Because of my allergies, I already knew I had a screwed-up immune system, so even if I had encountered an opportunity to try any of them, I would never have done so for fear it would trigger some kind of allergic reaction.

We held our party outside so we wouldn't mess up the house— and we had a ball! Sox had built a stereo from a kit, and he brought it over to play records on. We danced a lot and played some parlor games. After the party, we policed the area *verrry* carefully to pick up all of the beer bottle caps and cigarette butts. When my parents got home, my mom knew immediately what had transpired. She saw the grass all beaten down, and she found a bottle cap and a cigarette butt or two. She was not at all pleased! I don't recall my punishment, but I remember getting a lecture on violating trust, etc.

One weekend that spring, I borrowed my mother's convertible and six of us—three girls and three boys, although we were not paired off—drove up to the Valle Grande for a picnic. A couple of miles before we got to the edge of the Valle, a mountain lion suddenly appeared on our right, heading straight for the road at full speed! As I slammed on the brakes, he jumped a fence and in one bound was in the middle of the road not three feet in front of the car! He took one more bound and was over the fence on the other side of the road. We were all so stunned we just sat palefaced and silent for a few minutes. I don't know about the others, but I could just visualize him landing in the car with us. That was scary!

When I graduated from high school I was too young (seventeen) to get a summer job working at the lab. I began the summer filling in for one of my classmates, Roy Martin, at a bookstore. Then I got a job working at Baskin-Robbins. However, after a few weeks of serving and eating ice cream, Mac made me an offer I couldn't refuse. He, another school friend, Doug Gardner, and I got jobs traveling around the state running a kiddy carnival on our own. We ran three rides—some sturdy fiberglass miniature Model-T Fords that kids could actually steer (this was long before go-carts had appeared in New Mexico), a six-bucket Ferris wheel, and a motorized full-size stagecoach. The owner—a security guard at Los Alamos—just joined us on some weekends with a pony ride. It was not financially rewarding, but I think it was the most fun I ever had during a summer vacation.

I think everyone, including myself, assumed I would become a physicist, although my parents never specifically pressured me in that direction. Until I spent the year in Paris, I never really contemplated any field of endeavor outside of math or the natural sciences. That year, I discovered that there were other possible occupations in the world. I found that I thrived on communicating with others and was intrigued by the cultural differences among people. This was a major reason I moved away from the natural sciences. I thought about all those years my father had been isolated in the lab, and how much he had missed in terms of interpersonal relationships with people other than fellow scientists. I didn't see how he could possibly have a good understanding of human nature given what I perceived as his limited experience in dealing with people of varying backgrounds, socioeconomic status, etc. Another reason for my shift was that I felt that if I went into physics, I would somehow always be in competition with my father—at least in the eyes of others—and that was a competition in which I did not wish to participate. On the other hand, I had to be a science major in order to work as a summer student in the lab, and I wanted very much to do so.

After looking at a number of schools, I decided on Colorado College (C.C.) in Colorado Springs. I registered as a science major, but my initial focus was not on my studies. The first year I was there, I established a chess club and a bridge club, and was president of both throughout my college years. Most of the students at C.C. came from very well-to-do families, and money was not a problem for them. I received an allowance of twenty-five dollars per month. That simply was not sufficient to get through the month, so I taught chess and bridge; gave chess exhibitions, playing up to two dozen games simultaneously; and sang in a folk group to supplement my income. I also played a lot of bridge for money for the same reason.

Before the end of my freshman year I began playing duplicate bridge, and a month after I graduated, my partner (who was only a freshman) and I took third place in the open pairs competition at the summer national tournament in Denver. That was the last serious game of bridge I played, but my partner went on to become a professional bridge player. One year, I believe he and his younger brother took third in the world championships.

The tension of the Cuban Missile Crisis in October of 1961 was such that, unless you lived it, you can't really appreciate what it was like. Having grown up in Los Alamos with our frequent evacuations and all, I may have been more sensitive to the situation than most people my age, but I felt like I had gone from the frying pan into the fire by choosing to attend college in Colorado Springs.

We, the residents of Los Alamos, had always been given to understand that Los Alamos was a prime target in the event of a nuclear warhead exchange with the USSR, but in reality Los Alamos did not constitute a short-term threat to anyone. The lab was not capable of developing new weapons systems in a matter of weeks, and it was unlikely that a major conflagration involving nuclear warheads would last much longer than that. Colorado Springs, on the other hand, was unquestionably a prime target in the event of such a conflict. As I recall, there was a B-52[1] base, but more than that, it was home to the Continental Air Defense Command at ENT Air Force Base—the precursor of the North American Air Defense Command (NORAD). I believe Cheyenne Mountain, the hardened secure headquarters of NORAD, was presently under construction. Thus, if there was a national nerve center for purposes of responding to a nuclear attack, Colorado Springs was it.

During those two weeks, it was not at all clear that we (the people of earth) would wake up each morning. I kept my feelings about the situation to myself at school, but during the crisis, studying seemed particularly superfluous. I figured that my father was likely to be kept abreast of the situation, so I called my folks about every day during that two-week period to get updates.

After my freshman year, I worked in the lab under group leader Tom Putnam for the summer. Remember him from when he coached little league? As I mentioned previously, his was one of a three-group consortium working on "Project Sherwood" constructing Scilla IV. Its 216 large oil-filled capacitors were intended to discharge simultaneously to two huge aluminum collector plates that were situated directly beneath the framework. We smoothed and polished those collector plates for weeks so they would hold high voltage. During my last week on the job, we thoroughly cleaned them with pure alcohol in preparation for its first real test. Every day that week we got high just breathing the fumes.

With the tremendous energy release generated by all of those capacitors, Scilla IV was intended to compress deuterium and tritium to increase their density and temperature sufficiently to generate energy in the form of heat. The hope was to generate more energy than was required to produce the reaction, but it was never successful. This continues to be the goal of controlled thermonuclear research, but according to my father we shouldn't count on "fusion energy" for at least another fifty years. Being the eternal optimist, I'm betting we'll get there in forty-five years or less.

The big demonstration of Scilla IV, held in front of a lot of important people, including some visiting Russian physicists, occurred a week after my last day on the job. I was told that a considerable number of the capacitors exploded and that there was oil everywhere! Had I still been there, I would have been on the cleanup crew.

During my work on Scilla IV, I had the opportunity to observe one of the first lasers being tested. It used a ruby to achieve "coherent" light. Usually, light waves travel in all directions, but with coherent light, all of the light waves travel in the same direction. We saw this thing cut through a razor blade and do other amazing things. We instantly realized the vast potential for industrial and military uses of lasers! In fact, I find it surprising that lasers have not been used more extensively by now.

My sophomore year I again registered as a science major, and the following summer I worked in CMR (chemistry and metallurgical research) at the lab. My job was to analyze film that recorded the effects of subatomic particles on various "targets" after the particles had been accelerated to nearly the speed of light in, of all things, an accelerator. As we were in close proximity to many radioactive substances, it was a prerequisite that we be fitted with gas masks. There were several different types, and we had to put one on, enter a chamber filled with banana gas, bend over, reach up, and do a couple of other things to determine if it fit snugly. The first three masks I tried on leaked when I bent over, and the banana gas was so potent I got violently sick to my stomach. It was such an unpleasant experience that I wasn't able to tolerate the smell of bananas until I was over forty. I still prefer not to smell them.

We also had to wear outfits that completely covered our clothes, and cloth booties over our shoes. In addition, we wore badges that recorded our level of radiation exposure each day. At quitting time, our radiation levels were checked, and if we exceeded the "safe" level, we had to stay away from the lab for a day or so.

In the halls of the CMR building there were alarm buttons about every fifty feet so that, if there were a radiation leak, everyone could be made aware of it immediately and evacuate the building. One day the alarm sounded. Everyone else went scurrying for the front door, but I found myself instinctively running in the other direction to see if I could render assistance at the site of the leak. Fortunately, someone had pressed the button by accident and there was no leak.

One Friday night that summer, Steve, Mac, and Sox came by and tapped on my bedroom window. It was late, but they wanted me to play tennis and drink with them. Without much arm-twisting, I got dressed, grabbed my racket, and went out with them. We drove up the old "pipeline road" and drank several kinds of warm liquor straight from the bottle. I only took one small swig of each, and they all tasted terrible. However, I had only had hard liquor twice before,[2] and it was enough to get me really dizzy.

Then we went to the tennis courts at Urban Park, turned on the lights, and began playing "tennis." I kept trying to get the guys to be quiet, but to no avail. A porch light went on across the street and I suggested that we leave, but I was voted down. Sure enough, in a few minutes a police car pulled up. The officer came over to the tennis court and proceeded to ask us, one by one, how old we were. One by one we said, "Twenty." Mac and I were lying, as we were only nineteen. I have no idea why I said twenty, but I guess I thought that it would put us all in the same boat even if the boat was sinking.

We were pleasantly surprised when the officer suggested that we go home because there had been a complaint about the noise. We appreciatively thanked him and left. Soon after I got back in bed, I lost my cookies, and the next morning I had a terrible hangover. My parents didn't say a word, but my dad had a knowing grin on his face, so I suspect they knew what happened from the smell.

My junior year, following an appendectomy, I took a semester off from school. In February, Mac and I went to Mexico with my parents for a prolonged vacation. I then spent several months traveling around the country playing chess. Thereafter, TA and I made a trip to California. After I returned to school in the fall, I was never again to spend a prolonged period of time in Los Alamos. However, my life's path would intersect with Los Alamos in some surprising ways over the years to come.

I had long since come to realize that growing up in Los Alamos was something truly special, but it wasn't until after a conversation I had with Jennifer Tuck in 1994[3] that I began to realize the full impact on me and others of having done so. I address these issues in the sequel to *The Atomic City*, provisionally entitled *Fallout*.

Postscript

In sharing some of my personal experiences, I have attempted to impart a sense of what it was like growing up in the Atomic City. Despite the fact that many of our fathers and some of our mothers were essentially absentee parents for a number of years, their endeavors provided us with many opportunities not afforded most children. It truly was an age of innocence for those of us of high school age and younger. We enjoyed an exceptionally secure, carefree, and in many ways privileged childhood.

The constancy of the "duty to job overrides all else" attitude of the times, and the heightened expectations of our parents (and the community) regarding the future accomplishments of their children undoubtedly prompted many to strive for, and some to fulfill, those expectations. One of my classmates, Sarah Eyestone, has become a highly successful artist and, I believe, is destined to be recognized as the next Georgia O'Keeffe. She recently sent me a note in which she said: "I was empowered by my childhood there. It was a given that we would have amazing lives as there was nobody we knew who didn't. I always felt special and also very lucky to be dipped from my gene pool and raised by a community of friends."

For many others, however, there was a price to be paid for that idyllic childhood. That same high level of expectation took its toll in many ways.

An exceptionally high percentage of the students whose fathers were scientists at Los Alamos for some portion of the time between

1943 and 1955—the "high stress period"—went on to college. I imagine that a relatively high percentage of these people obtained advanced degrees. I further suspect that a relatively high percentage of those who obtained advanced degrees subsequently eschewed the field of their academic training to pursue unrelated endeavors.

I believe that many of us whose fathers were Los Alamos scientists have subsequently had difficulty finding contentment in life, at least in part because of the strong undercurrent of urgency and importance of the work being done at the Atomic City during and after World War II. Every task was not only important, it was vital that each objective be achieved as quickly as possible—first to beat the Germans to the punch, and later to keep the Russians from catching up with us. I'm sure I was not alone in my perception that this was the sort of thing that gave life true meaning. These were not the mere musings of children fresh from reading the newest Superman comic book; rather, they derived from years of seeing our elders working furiously, engaged in a life-and-death struggle of global consequence—and succeeding! As a result, I suspect that many of us have experienced difficulties in forging lasting marital relationships and have experienced emotional and/or stress-related maladies in numbers that would be considered excessive given the "carefree" nature of our childhood. As they pertain to Jennifer Tuck and myself, these issues will be addressed in the sequel to this book, provisionally entitled *Fallout*.

The sequel not only looks at some of the impacts that growing up in Los Alamos has had on Jennifer, me, and perhaps others. It includes a review of a number of the trials and tribulations I encountered later in life, such as my battle with, and victory (to date) over, multiple sclerosis. It glances at my several failed marriages and numerous other personal relationships. It looks back at some of the more personal and humorous aspects of my early years, my years in college and in law school, and my careers. Finally, it elucidates my late-blossoming relationship with Jennifer Tuck—the first relationship with a woman I had ever experienced that I truly believed would last until I died—the tragic accident that took her life in 1999, and my struggle to deal with that loss. As I mentioned previously, from the age of about thirteen it was always in the back of my mind that Jennifer and I would somehow, someday, be together. Little did I know that it would be nearly forty years before it happened. In 1997, despite her being aware of my heart and lung problems, Jennifer decided to move to Denver to be with me, and we spent the last twenty-one months of her life together until her untimely and tragic death on April 30, 1999. Those months were the happiest of my adult life, and Jennifer often told me they were the happiest of hers, as well.

General Leslie Groves, circa 1944.
—Photo courtesy of Los Alamos National Laboratory

The Valle Grande is one of the largest calderas (craters created by the collape of volcanoes) in the world. The caldera's main valley is up to eight miles wide and fourteen miles long, circa 1990.

—Photo by Jennifer Tuck

Robert Oppenheimer, circa 1944.
——Photo courtesy of Los Alamos National Laboratory

The Old Otowi Bridge, circa 2000.

—Photo by Terry Rosen

Post Exchange, circa 1944.

—Photographer unknown

The Front Gate, circa 1955.
—Photo courtesy of Los Alamos National Laboratory

Ashley Pond, circa 1945.
—Photo courtesy of Los Alamos National Laboratory

"Building the Bridge," circa 1950.
—Photo courtesy of Los Alamos National Laboratory

The lab, circa 1945.
—Photo courtesy of Los Alamos National Laboratory

Los Alamos ("Project Y"), circa 1945. (* marks our "Sundt").
—Photo courtesy of Los Alamos National Laboratory

Fuller Lodge, circa 1943.
—Photographer unknown

Fuller Lodge, 1999.

—Photo by Terry Rosen

The "Big House," circa 1943.

—Photographer unknown

Hans Bethe, circa 1945.
—Photo courtesy of Los Alamos National Laboratory

Enrico Fermi, circa 1945.
—Photo courtesy of Los Alamos National Laboratory

Stan Ulam, circa 1945.
—Photo courtesy of Los Alamos National Laboratory

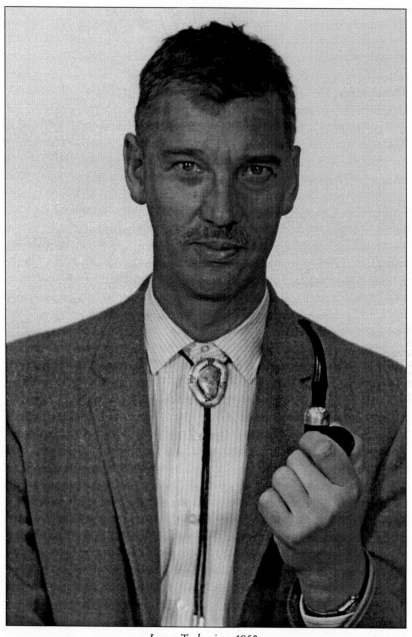

James Tuck, circa 1950.

—Photographer unknown

Norris Bradbury, circa 1970.
—Photo courtesy of Los Alamos National Laboratory

Left to right: Dr. Peterson (visitor or consultant), Edward Teller, and Norris Bradbury, circa 1945.

—Photo courtesy of Los Alamos National Laboratory

Exterior of Los Alamos Neutron Science Center (LANSCE), circa 1980.

—Photo courtesy of Los Alamos National Laboratory.

Interior of LAMPF, a.k.a. LANSCE, circa 1980.

The Ranch School Icehouse was used as the first depository of fissionable material in Los Alamos, circa 1944.

—Photo courtesy of Los Alamos National Laboratory

E. O. Lawrence Award and medal: Dr. Louis Rosen was one of five scientists presented with the E. O. Lawrence Award in 1963. One of the medals is on display in the Smithsonian Institution.

—Photo by Terry Rosen

Helen Cordero and granddaughter Buffy, circa 1972.

—Photo by Mary Rosen

Louis and Mary Rosen, circa 1942.

—Photographer unknown

Louis and Mary Rosen, 1989.

—Photographer unknown

Zozobra, circa 2000.

—Photo by Lisa Law

"Winter's Solace," circa 1994.

—Photo by Terry Rosen

STAR WRITING™: "A Thousand Words," 1995.

—Photo by Terry Rosen

STAR WRITING™: The Atomic City.
See Appendix IV for explanation.

—Photo by Terry Rosen

Epilogue

In May 2000, a horrendous forest fire ravaged Los Alamos. The so-called "Cerro Grande" fire took up to 1,500 firefighters nearly a month to extinguish. Over 250 structures were destroyed and more than 400 families were left homeless. Ironically, the "controlled (prescribed) burn" was started intentionally on May 4 by the National Park Service to reduce the risk of forest fires. The National Weather Service had advised against starting the fire. The forest was extremely dry, humidity was low, high winds were expected, and there was no relief in sight. After burning for ten days, the fire was only 5 percent contained and had caused over a billion dollars in damage. It took three weeks just to get the fire fully contained. However, it did achieve its primary objective. There is unlikely to be a forest fire in the area in the forseeable future because there is no underbrush left to burn. The end, though, obviously did not justify the means.

There have been a number of forest fires around Los Alamos over the years, some of which have posed serious threats to the lab and the town. At times, as I mentioned previously, even the scientists (including my father) manned the fire lines. However, I believe this is the first time such a fire has actually damaged any significant structures.

I always believed that, due of the importance of the work being done at Los Alamos, the government would prevent any harm from coming to the lab or the town at all costs. Unfortunately, as I got older, I never updated my childhood perception that our government can do anything it sets its mind to. Consequently, when I heard that this fire had reached the town, I had a hard time coming to grips with the idea. Although the lab and the town's residents were successfully evacuated, for days we did not know whether my parents' home had survived the fire. During that time, I felt as though I was adrift in an ocean with nothing to hold on to but a piece of driftwood.

I have lived in many residences, and it would have been upsetting if any of them had been destroyed. I would have mourned the loss not of the TV, but of the irreplaceable mementos, such as photos of friends and loved ones. Oh, and there's that Cub Scout shirt. However, the very idea of my parents' home being destroyed was deeply disturbing to me. If I live to be 100, that house will still be "home." I felt a sense of enormous impending loss—precious artifacts of an era of special historical significance with which the homes of my parents and other wartime residents are replete.

Had this fire occurred during the 1950s, the loss would have been almost forgotten in a few years thanks to the indomitable "Los Alamos Spirit." However, those people are now in their late seventies or older, and starting over is not a viable option. Insurance cannot replace a lifetime of mementos from travels around the world. It cannot replace the storyteller doll that Helen Cordero made especially for my mother. It cannot replace the hundreds of little things that renew old memories. Some of the homes that burned did belong to people of my parents' generation, and I grieve for their loss.

In mid-May 1980, authorities ordered the evacuation of residents in the environs of Mount St. Helens because the volcano was expected to erupt at any time. One man, Harry Truman, refused to evacuate. During the Cerro Grande fire, Los Alamos had several Harry Trumans of its own. Fortunately, they did not suffer the same fate as Mount St. Helens' Harry Truman. He was buried under mud and debris when the volcano erupted.

Many people have come to distrust the federal government over the years. Whatever the reasons, this fire fostered a deeper level of distrust. During the Cerro Grande fire, the government of New Mexico set up its own radiation monitoring system because it didn't trust the federal government to accurately report the results of its monitoring system. I find that both interesting and disturbing.

However, despite the confidence-cracking damage done by the Cerro Grande fire, it did not succeed in destroying the "Los Alamos Spirit." Nor did it diminish the ability of the laboratory to carry out its vital functions. Los Alamos National Laboratory remains a world-class scientific research facility of critical importance to the security of the United States.

On August 13, 2000, the *Santa Fe New Mexican*—the newspaper with the largest circulation in New Mexico outside of the Albuquerque dailies—published a "letter to the editor" that was highly critical of New Mexico Senator Pete Dominici and of the endeavors of LANL over the years. It suggested that the people of Los Alamos deserved what they got with the Cerro Grande fire. My father, concerned about the morale of lab employees, especially since it had taken such a drubbing lately from the fire, submitted a response to the local newspaper—the *Los Alamos Monitor*—which promptly published it. Senator Dominici read both letters and called my father to encourage him to submit his letter to the *Santa Fe New Mexican*. My father accommodated the senator's request, and the *New Mexican* reprinted it.[1]

That letter, along with other of my father's writings over the years, presages the energy crisis that enveloped California in 2001 and threatens the rest of the country. In so doing, it punctuates the folly of not pursuing the broader use of nuclear energy.

Shortly after *The Atomic City* went to press, the following announcement was made:

> The 2002 Los Alamos National Laboratory Medal award recipients are [Laboratory Senior Fellow Emeritus] Louis Rosen and . . . George Cowan.
>
> The Los Alamos National Medal, instituted in 2001, is the highest honor the Laboratory can bestow on an individual. . . . The first recipients of the award were Nobel Laureate Hans Bethe and former Laboratory Director Harold Agnew.
>
> Rosen will receive the medal in recognition of his outstanding scientific contributions to the Laboratory and to the nation. . . . His work as a Laboratory leader, a community leader

and a national leader have brought great distinction to the Laboratory . . .

Conspicuous by its absence is the lack of any mention in this book of the world-renowned Albuquerque Balloon Festival. The reason is that it wasn't conceived until 1972. My parents attended the first one, and they have told me that there were three balloons at the event. Currently, the number of balloons is approaching 2,000. Now, that's inflation!

Appendix I

Chemical vs. Fission vs. Fusion Bombs

When you start a fire in the fireplace, the burning wood releases energy in the form of light and heat. The primary difference between a burning log and a chemical bomb (e.g. TNT) is the rate of ignition of the combustible material. In both cases, the end products (i.e. smoke and ashes) have slightly less mass than the initial reactants (i.e. wood and oxygen). The amount of energy released in the combustion process and in the detonation of all bombs—chemical and nuclear—is determined by Einstein's formula $E = mc^2$. E (energy) = m (the change in mass) multiplied by c (speed of light) squared.

In a fission (atomic) bomb, the energy release results from splitting nuclei of atoms of uranium or plutonium. The resulting energy release is about 1 million times more efficient than that achieved in the combustion process of a chemical bomb. Thus, a fission bomb containing one hundred pounds of uranium releases approximately 1 million times more energy than a chemical bomb of the same weight.

In a fusion (hydrogen, or "H") bomb, the energy release comes from combining the nuclei of atoms, resulting in a net loss in mass. H-bombs convert mass to energy about five times more efficiently than do A-bombs. However, the primary reason H-bombs are so much more powerful than A-bombs is that an A-bomb cannot exceed a certain mass without self-destructing (pre-detonating), whereas there is no such limit on the size of an H-bomb.

Appendix II

Awards Bestowed upon Louis Rosen, Ph.D.

- Fellow of the American Physical Society
- Fellow of the American Association for the Advancement of Science
- Guggenheim Fellowship (1959)
- E. O. Lawrence Award and Medal (1963)
- Golden Plate Award of the American Academy of Achievement (1964)
- New Mexico Citizen of the Year, bestowed by the New Mexico Realtors Association, and Distinguished Citizen of the Year, awarded by the Los Alamos Chamber of Commerce (both in 1973)
- New Mexico Distinguished Public Service Award (1978)
- Alumni Fellow of Penn State University (1978)
- Honorary Doctor of Science Degree from the University of New Mexico (1979)
- Sesquicentennial (150-year) Honorary Professor of the University of Alabama (1981)
- Member of the Board of Governors, Tel Aviv University (1985–86)
- Senior Fellow of Los Alamos National Laboratory (1985)
- Honorary Doctor of Science Degree from the University of Colorado (1987)
- Senior Fellow, Emeritus, of the Los Alamos National Laboratory (LANL) (1991)
- The Los Alamos Medal (2002)

Appendix III

Louis Rosen's Letter to the Editor[1]

The Cerro Grande fire disaster catalyzed a remarkable outpouring of kindness, compassion and generosity, dramatically strengthening the historically tepid bond between Los Alamos and its adopted state. But it appears that this tragedy also stimulated some who have made a career of opposing all things nuclear, especially nuclear deterrence and, of course, nuclear energy and nuclear-produced radiation (other than sunlight).

Why is it that the critics of the nuclear age can ignore the enormous benefits this development has brought to our civilization? The development of nuclear technology was unavoidable. Fortunately it was developed first under democratic institutions.

It ended World War II, saving enormous numbers of lives on both sides. Nuclear weapons have arguably deterred war involving the major world powers for 55 years, the longest such interval in modern history.

It is now all but certain that global warming, fueled by the "greenhouse effect," is with us. Burning fossil fuels is hazardous to our health and to the environment. Oil reserves are diminishing and our dependence on imports poses a danger to our military and economic security, not to mention international stability. Nuclear energy can be the solution to this dilemma. We are today facing significant shortfalls of electricity. Not so in France and Japan. Most of their electricity comes from nuclear reactors, which are now safe, reliable and affordable. But the above is just the tip of the benefits iceberg. Today millions of people each year are diagnosed and treated using nuclear particles or radiation from radioactive nuclei produced in accelerators and reactors. Radiation is used to protect air travelers and to protect all of us from dangerous bacteria in the food chain. It is used to increase safety and efficiency in production of goods of every description.

I, too, would welcome a world devoid of weapons of mass destruction nuclear, biological and chemical. However, in the absence of verifiable, worldwide disarmament, unilateral nuclear disarmament by the world's superpower would, in my opinion, constitute reckless endangerment of national security and international security.

In the light of recent history and the potential shortages of energy, food and water in the future, who can guarantee that no nation will try to use nuclear, biological or chemical blackmail to impose its will on others? Even so we have halted the testing of nuclear weapons, and we are reducing our stockpile.

The mission of LANL and other nuclear weapons laboratories is not self-determining. It is mandated by the U.S. Congress. These laboratories are a national security insurance policy of enormous value. They also contribute greatly to the science and technology base which gives rise to improvements in our quality of life. So why are these institutions being vilified? Is it based on disinformation, misinformation, ignorance or simply the need for some of us to have a "cause" which engenders fear or anger?

A case in point (a relatively moderate one) is the Aug. 13 Perspective article in the "New Mexican" entitled "A New Legacy for DOE, LANL and Dominici." The author chastises our senior senator for the nature of his contribution to the economy of New Mexico.

The article states, "perhaps the entire strand upon which he has dedicated himself, the promotion of the nuclear industry is outmoded, dangerous, and counterproductive." The author is not concerned that by mid-century our nation, as well as much of the world, will be in dire need of nuclear energy, and we know from the past that it takes 50 years to safely bring up a new energy source into the world economy. For a nuclear energy economy, safety in production and operation is paramount.

My family and I came to New Mexico in 1944. We saw a state with unmatched beauty in its environment and its people. But we also saw extreme poverty on a large scale, inaccessible health care and grossly inadequate education.

It is to the credit of great leaders like the late Senator Anderson and today's Sen. Domenici that the state has advanced so dramatically during the past century.

So what is it that propels the author of subject article to state "I challenge Sen. Domenici to take a fresh look at his leadership agenda and consider that his legacy, up until this point, will go down in history as a machiavellian effort to lay waste the state that he is supposed to have represented." The author wants Sen. Domenici to issue "a call for an all-out national effort for scientists to reverse or neutralize radioactive material."

So what can I say other than the following: Scientists do not possess, as far as I am aware, supernatural power. They cannot repeal the laws of nature. However, they can and do work to mitigate unwelcome byproducts of technology. They have, in fact, found a way to reduce the radioactivity that is the byproduct of nuclear energy.

It is called ATW (accelerator transmutation of nuclear waste). This process can proceed in parallel with production of electric power. This research is underway in a number of laboratories worldwide, including LANL where I believe it started, thanks to the strong support of Sen. Domenici.

Appendix IV

About STAR WRITING™

In the summer of 1993, I began experimenting with astro-photography—the science and art of taking pictures of the stars, planets, meteors, and other night-sky activities[2]—in part to try to lower my elevated blood pressure. I figured it would be a calm, low-stress activity. I rented lenses of various focal lengths and took numerous photos of the moon, planets, and stars. My experiments gave me an understanding of proper exposure times, and of how difficult it is to get, and keep, heavenly bodies in sharp focus.

In early 1994, I read about the impending collision of more than twenty segments of the comet Shoemaker-Levy with Jupiter. I was fascinated with the idea of seeing and photographing a change in a "heavenly body" as it occurred—a cosmic event which I believed was unprecedented in history.[3] I contacted the Gates Planetarium to ask if they would allow me to photograph the impacts of Shoemaker-Levy on Jupiter using their telescope and my camera.

The planetarium agreed, with the understanding that they could have whatever photos they wanted for educational purposes. I immediately began reading up on astrophotography. The first item I read began with, "Astrophotography is, by far, the most difficult field of photography." After a big gulp, I continued reading and began to practice. Despite my blood pressure concerns, I had managed to put myself back in a pressure-filled situation.

When the big event arrived (July 16–22, 1994) I was still in a steep learning curve, but I shot five rolls of film and was delighted with the results! Jupiter was focused as clearly in my photos as it was in the images projected for the public to view at Gates Planetarium. Furthermore, and this is the really exciting part, my photos actually showed a couple of the impact disturbances created by the impacts on Jupiter.

That experience inspired me to continue with astrophotography, but after Shoemaker-Levy, everything else seemed anti-climactic. As I continued to photograph star trails I began to think, "There must be something more that can be done with astrophotography; some way to use the stars as a vehicle for artistic expression and communication." With much experimentation, the concept of STAR WRITING™ evolved.

I jokingly point out that I am not only the world's foremost expert on STAR WRITING™. I am the world's *only* expert because no one else has ever done it. However, I hope that with the dawning of public awareness and the potential that STAR WRITING™ offers for artistic expression, other "experts" will evolve.

STAR WRITING™ has been referred to as a "scientific art." I consider this a bit of an overstatement. STAR WRITING™ is simply a mix of astrophotography, basic math, art, and patience. It is a new photographic technique that provides a unique forum for artistic expression by combining the "motion of the stars across the sky" with the Morse Code to spell out words. This is achieved by covering and uncovering the camera lens at specific intervals while creating time-lapse photos of star trails.

If you are interested in knowing more about STAR WRITING™, write to STAR WRITING, Inc.; P.O. Box 8796; Denver, CO 80201-8796 and enclose $5 to cover costs of printing and mailing. You will also receive a 4"x6" sample of STAR WRITING™ and a price list for available STAR WRITING™ images in the event that you would like to own one. If you are interested in having Mr. Rosen create a custom STAR WRITING™ image for you, call 303-692-8891. Note that the minimum fee for a custom image is $500.

STAR WRITING™ Images Produced as of 2000

TITLE
STAR TRAILS (Pre-Star Writ.)
 AMAZING GRACE
A THOUSAND WORDS
FAMILY IS FOREVER
FREEDOM
GOD BLESS AMERICA
GOD IS
GOOD FRIENDS ARE
   FOREVER
GO AVALANCHE
GO BRONCOS
GO BUFFS
GO NUGGETS
GO ROCKIES
HAPPY ANNIVERSARY
HAPPY BIRTHDAY
HAPPY BIRTHDAY DAD
HAPPY BIRTHDAY MOM
HAPPY HOLIDAYS
HAPPY NEW YEAR
HAPPY VALENTINES DAY
I LOVE YOU
INFINITE LOVE
INFINITY
I THINK THEREFORE I AM
IT IS WRITTEN
JUSTICE
LET FREEDOM RING
LIVE AND LOVE LIFE
MERRY CHRISTMAS
PEACE ON EARTH (+ airplane trail)
PEACE ON EARTH
SHOOT FOR THE STARS
STAR TRAILS
STAR WRITING
STOP THE VIOLENCE

SUCCESS IS HAPPINESS
   IS SUCCESS
THANK YOU
TO BE IS TO DO
TO BE OR NOT TO BE
   THAT IS THE QUESTION
TO DO IS TO BE
TRUTH
TRUTH AND JUSTICE
WE ARE ONE
Y2K

ASTROLOGICAL SIGNS
AQUARIUS
AIRES*
CANCER*
CAPRICORN
GEMINI*
LEO*
LIBRA*
PISCES
SAGITTARIUS
SCORPIO*
TAURUS*
VIRGO

NAMES
ANTHONY HOPKINS
ELVIS PRESLEY
JOHN ELWAY
JOHN WAYNE
SOPHIA LOREN

GEOGRAPHIC LOCATIONS
DENVER
LAS VEGAS

*Image repeated in different direction.

Notes

About the Author

1. STAR WRITING™ is explained in Appendix IV.
2. Note that Jennifer and "Polly" Tuck are one and the same person. Jim and Elsie Tuck adopted her in 1947 when she was three weeks old. They named her Sarah, but nicknamed her Polly. In 1997 she located her birth mother and learned that her original given name was Jennifer, so she had her name legally changed to Jennifer.

Chapter 1

1. Derived from Richard Rhodes, *The Making of the Atomic Bomb*, Simon and Schuster, New York, 1986, p.490.
2. For a rudimentary explanation of the differences between chemical, fission (atomic), and fusion (thermonuclear, a.k.a. hydrogen) bombs, see Appendix I.
3. En route to and from these rides, Oppie often stayed the night in Cundiyo, a little town where every resident was related to the Vijil family—this according to Fabiola Baca, who worked as a maid for the Bradburys, the Rosens, and many other longtime residents of Los Alamos.
4. The Valle Grande is a giant crater resulting from the collapse of volcanoes. See photo page 154.
5. By the end of the war, the population of Project Y was 4,700, including hundreds of scientists.
6. Richard Rhodes, *The Making of the Atomic Bomb*, p.451.
7. Edward Teller, "The Nuclear Dynamo—Can A Nuclear Tornado Annihilate Nations?" *Fusion Technology*, Vol. 19, January 1991, p. 163. This article was received Oct. 7, 1988, and accepted for publication January 29, 1990.
8. G. Breit, Notes for talk on Atmospheric Ignition, fall of 1952.
9. Edward Teller, "The Nuclear Dynamo," p. 165.

Chapter 2
1. Some of the information about Edith Warner was derived from *The House at Otowi Bridge,* by Peggy Pond Church, University of New Mexico Press, Albuquerque, NM, 1960.
2. *Frijoles* (pronounced free-HO-lays) is Spanish for "beans." The canyon's name derived from the conclusion of archeologists that the Indians who lived there grew a lot of beans.
3. Prefabricated houses assembled by Robert McKee.
4. Houses constructed by Mr. Sundt.

Chapter 3
1. The encryption is in honor of Dick Feynman.
2. The neutron is the component of the nucleus that is the key to nuclear energy production on earth.
3. Richard Rhodes, *The Making of the Atomic Bomb,* p.449. This book earned Rhodes a Pulitzer Prize.
4. Glen Seaborg, working with Emelio Segré, first identified plutonium^{239} in late 1941.
5. George Gamow is well known for his authorship of numerous books on physics that are written so a layperson can understand them. An example is his ever-popular *One, Two, Three, Infinity.*
6. Rubby Sherr was a professor at Princeton before the war.
7. I understand that Seth actually championed the implosion concept long before anyone knew that it was the *only* way to get the plutonium bomb to work.
8. This is not a typo. Computers did not yet exist, so computing had to be done using mechanical calculators.
9. Michael Smith, *Station X,* Boxtree, United Kingdom, 1998, p. 227.
10. Richard Rhodes, *The Making of the Atomic Bomb,* p. 452.
11. Robert Bacher (born 1905) was wartime director of G (Gadget)-Division. "Gadget" was the code name for the first plutonium bomb, dubbed "Fat Man."
12. Otto Hahn and Fritz Strassman (and, independently, Enrico Fermi) had created nuclear fission but had misinterpreted the results. It was Meitner and Frisch who figured out that fission had occurred, and Frisch coined the phrase "nuclear fission," based on the term used to describe the division of protozoa. Niels Bohr made the announcement at the meeting in Washington.
13. Taschek was alternate P-Division leader under Jerry Kellogg, and my father was alternate P-Division leader with Taschek for about a year until MP-(Meson Physics) Division was established in 1966.
14. The name was changed to Los Alamos National Laboratory (LANL) on January 1, 1981, and it will be referred to hereafter as LANL.

Chapter 4
1. John Allred was working toward his doctorate in physics under the guidance of my father.
2. Reprinted with permission of *The Santa Fe New Mexican.*
3. Parenthetical expression added.

4. Louis Rosen, Ph.D., "Los Alamos now on nuclear energy side of freedom," *Santa Fe New Mexican,* June 25, 1970, page 5, col. 1.
5. Ibid, col. 3
6. Louis Rosen, Ph.D., "Los Alamos now on nuclear energy side of freedom," *Santa Fe New Mexican,* June 25, 1970, page 6, col. 4.
7. Whether the vice premier intentionally reversed the "round" and the "square" is not clear.
8. For additional information on Louis Rosen, see Appendix II and consult *Who's Who in America, American Men of Science,* and McGraw-Hill's *Modern Scientists and Engineers* (1981).

Chapter 5
1. Headlines from the front page of the August 6, 1945, issue of *The Santa Fe New Mexican.* All segments are reprinted with the permission of *The Santa Fe New Mexican.*
2. *The Santa Fe New Mexican,* June 25, 1970, page 1, col. 2-3, top to middle.
3. William McNulty, *Santa Fe New Mexican,* June 25, 1970, page 1, col. 2-5, bottom.
4. Two letters of this word were illegible.
5. *The Santa Fe New Mexican,* June 25, 1970, page 1, cols. 6-8.
6. All of my other sources indicate that the limit was actually fifty or seventy-five miles, and they all agree that Albuquerque, which is one hundred miles from Los Alamos, was beyond the allowable limit.
7. *The Santa Fe New Mexican,* June 25, 1970, page D9.
8. Ibid., page D10, col. 2.
9. The Russians entered the war against Japan just before the first atomic bomb was used on Hiroshima. Thus, some Japanese were concerned that, if surrender had been delayed, the Russians would have had greater opportunity to devour parts of Japan.

Chapter 6
1. Creator unknown.
2. See photo on page 170.
3. The first Santa Fe Fiesta dates back to 1712.

Chapter 7
1. Criticality is the point at which fissionable material begins a self-sustaining chain reaction.
2. Otto Frisch, *What Little I Remember,* Cambridge University Press, Cambridge, 1980, p. 171.
3. William Shirer, *The Rise and Fall of the Third Reich,* Simon and Schuster, New York, 1960, p. 224.

Chapter 8
1. Tom Putnam was working with Project Sherwood when I worked there in 1962.

2. As I recall, the results of those early studies showed that the level of radiation present in residents of Los Alamos was no higher than in other people who live at that altitude.

Chapter 9
1. Actually, I spent my junior year in Paris, France, and TA's family moved to Albuquerque during the senior year. However, TA returned to Los Alamos to graduate with the rest of us.
2. STAR WRITING™ is explained in Appendix IV.
3. *The Santa Fe New Mexican,* October 24, 1956 (page unknown)
4. Ibid.
5. An arroyo is a big ditch that has water in it only when it rains higher up in the mountains.
6. I believe that Kent was the first person from Los Alamos to attend the U.S. Air Force Academy, which had been established just a few years earlier.

Chapter 11
1. The B-52 long-range bomber was the centerpiece of the United States' nuclear weapon delivery capability at the time. To ensure that they would not be eliminated by a pre-emptive Soviet air and/or missile strike, a force of armed B-52s were in the air twenty-four hours a day, seven days a week, for many years.
2. There was that hot-buttered rum when I was ten. Then, when I was about thirteen, after a long, hot pickup basketball game, I chugged a large glass of what I thought was lemonade which turned out to be daiquiris.
3. This was the first time we had talked in over thirty years, but it led to us spending the rest of her life together. This is addressed in depth in *Fallout.*

Epilogue
1. See Appendix III for a copy of the letter to the editor.

Appendices
1. Authored by Louis Rosen, Ph.D., this letter was published in the *Los Alamos Monitor* on August 18, 2000, and, subsequently, in *The Santa Fe New Mexican.*
2. As defined by physicist and science fiction author Isaac Asimov.
3. I have since learned that astronomer Guiseppi Bruno allegedly observed an impact on the moon in the late sixteenth century. A moon crater bears his name.

Index